JILL OUT THE BOX

...HEART MATTERS

A Unique Book
by
Jilean D. Fabien

JILL OUT THE BOX-Heart Matters

This title is also available as a Kindle e-book.
Visit www.amazon.com

All scripture quotations, unless otherwise indicated are taken from the Holy Bible, New King James Version.

Printed in the United States of America by:
Kindle Direct Publishing

First Printing April 2020

ISBN-13: 978-976-95780-3-6

E-Book ISBN: 978-976-95780-4-3

Published by:
JOTBox Ltd.
66 Faralon Drive, Bel-Air,
La Romaine, Trinidad and Tobago
E-mail: jotboxltd@gmail.com

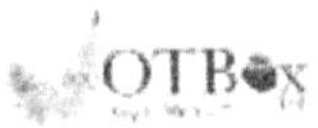

DEDICATION

This book is dedicated to everyone who has ever felt hopeless or disempowered…to anyone who has given up on a dream or asked, "Why am I here?"

ACKNOWLEDGEMENTS

I am eternally grateful to my Heavenly Father without whom, it would not have been possible to write. For, it is a collective of my experiences on my life's journey to purpose and destiny with Him, the wisdom gained and lessons learnt. He has gifted me as a scribe to be able to share these nuggets with you. It is my hope that your life would never be the same after taking this journey, if even the change is as small as a mustard seed.

Special thanks as well to my brother, Jesus, whose ultimate life sacrifice has enabled me to reconnect with our Father, My Creator, the Source of my purpose and experience a love, freedom and fulfillment that I had not known prior to our encounter.

To my 'Out the Box' husband, Errol who provided much inspiration and sacrificed in countless ways for this book to be birthed, and who supported me tirelessly, "Thank you" could never adequately express my heart matter. God has given you a special grace...You exemplify His love in my life.

To Chilo, my son who has shown a strength and wisdom far beyond his years throughout the journey that has brought us to this point. There were many times when your hugs and "I Love You Mummy" gave me the strength to continue. Thank you for being a trooper, your small things were big with God and me.

To my Mom, Dad and my siblings for all the things that parents and siblings do, including the banter and questioning. I'm forever grateful for all you've instilled in me and for your support and sacrifice, even when you didn't understand my walk at times. What a priceless gift a loving family is! My family of origin has served to shape my life in such an invaluable way and helped me to find my place in the world.

My 'Women out the Box,' you've supported me over the years as my other sisters, my friends and inner circle, thank you for allowing God to use you in my life, especially Kimmy, Michelle E, Cindy B, Teju, Bev J, Jacqui H, Carla R, Aliya, Shé B, Crissy, KK Streets, Nicole P, Marva, Celine, Terry-Ann, Trines and Lana. You are priceless gifts to me. I need 'The Space' just as much as you do.

Special thanks to Mr. Arthur Dunk of the Caribbean Bone Marrow Registry who extended himself to my first husband and me at a time of 'life or death' and who showed his support and blessed Chilo and me in numerous ways thereafter. His work is changing the world and giving life and hope to many with Leukemia.

Thank you to those of you who challenged my faith, laughed, mocked, betrayed or maligned me. Know that I have forgiven you and that all of it has served to drive me into deeper relationship with my Father and broke my heart to cause me to truly love and manifest the purpose He placed in me.

ENDORSEMENTS

Heart Matters is a relatable, honest expression. It addresses many of the questions we often wrestle with in our daily walk. Jilean's real life experiences and gifted insight can assist those desiring to honour God in their relationships. Her commitment to the life-changing principles found in God's word is encouraging as we get a glimpse into how God blesses obedience and grants us the desires of our heart.

Kim Colthrust
Administrator/ Educator/ Friend

This 'Unique Book' was indeed full of surprises. I've never read anything like it. I found myself connecting with it on different levels...professionally, personally and purposefully. I rediscovered some of my forgotten and neglected chambers. 'Jill Out the Box' dares to go where many would be afraid to.

Garfield Victor
Executive Chef

I had to restart several times as I got so drawn in and lost in the story that I forgot I was supposed to be reading with an Editor's eye. I enjoyed the material and stopped a few times to pray and ask God to be merciful to me as well. Conversion all around, I guess.

Michelle Ellis
Owner/Director, Matty's Inn/
Founder, Wonder Woman Events/Editor

"Jill Out the Box- Heart Matters" offers a deeply reflective, highly inspirational and brutally honest experience through the eyes of a believer. The book is a sincere invitation to join in a miraculous adventure along a path to self-understanding through the exploration of every aspect of one's being, through the source of our being. Heart Matters is an act of charity, a gift of knowledge, knowing, truth and Love.

Wendy Augustus
Executive Director-Tertiary Level Institution

Simple, transformative, provocation of every religiously rooted fibre..." Jill Out the Box- Heart Matters" is a life living, daring you to turn the next page. Sometimes, joy, curiosity, anger...other times, sobbing through the flowing lines and clinching-taking a much-needed moment to reflect and dig into the understanding of what I just read. "Did she actually say that!" Excellent chronicles. I encourage...no I dare you to plunge in.

Andre Antonio
Mentor/Friend

TABLE OF CONTENTS

A NOTE TO MY READERS

Thank you for opening yourself to me by purchasing this book. It's always special when people give a mustard seed about what I have to say or give their hard-earned finances in exchange for something I've produced.

I guarantee this book is unlike any other you've read before. It is not a scholarly work and follows no particular structure or style. It's just written as I was guided to write it, very much in a flow. It is not written in chronological order. It includes actual conversations with God, verses and songs written years ago, and some that happened in the moment, my stories and testimonies.

I suppose that's why JOTBox *had to publish it because not many would have been willing to take the chance or be open to the criticism that will come.*

It is my hope that you'll be inspired, set free, empowered, even offended and that your heart would never be the same after reading.

As Paul said, so do I,

"And my speech and my preaching were not with persuasive words of human wisdom, but in demonstration of the Spirit and of power…" 1 Corinthians 2:4

HEART TO HEART CONVERSATION

I am at a loss for words...it feels as though my heart is being pulled and tugged in many directions, and I'm confused as to what you're doing Lord.

I didn't know what You meant when You said that You were going to do a deep healing of my heart. I didn't object or doubt, but I wasn't aware of any heart issues. Then came the trials and the processing...it's amazing how much we gain when we lack.

My current financial situation has drawn me into a deeper place with You, and in the depths of this ocean, I've found chambers of my heart I hadn't realised were closed to You. In the depths of this place, I've found purposes I hadn't yet thought of, and some that had drowned. You've been drawing everything out of me. Out of this death, You're breathing new life, resurrecting forgotten dreams and generating new streams.

Everything must die in order for You to make it abundantly fruitful, including me. Resurrection power could not be made manifest in a live vessel.

UNLOCKING CHAMBER 1

When You started the healing work, You said that You wanted me to communicate with You about my emotions and that You care about what I feel, even though You're moved by my faith? I stopped talking, and this is why I've been feeling distant emotionally. I've been in a space for so long where I've had to function in obedience only and not emotion because I would not have been able to survive otherwise.

There was no one else who would have understood or who could have caressed me at that time, so I just stopped sharing, since I knew what You wanted me to do.

Now, You're bringing healing to my heart and smoothing the feathers that were damaged in the process of coming through the storms.

So, here I am talking...

UNLOCKING CHAMBER 2

I remember a time when I had 'out the box' faith...the kind where I would look and sound foolish to people and appear to be living in a bubble of my own. I actually was living in my own world- the Kingdom of Faith. When I believed for something, it was settled, and I behaved as though it was already true.

Somewhere along the way, I didn't see the manifestation of things as I'd believed, and I stopped stepping out in the way I used to because 'deferred hope' made my heart very sick. I didn't want to set myself up for anymore disappointment. I thought my heart couldn't take anymore.

So, I gave everything up and figured You would do what You wanted, when you wanted. I don't think I was angry with You, but I think I became very apathetic. You are sovereign and Your timing is perfect Lord. On the real though, I realise now that I've been disappointed because I've been living by faith and not seeing the results in the measure I'd expected. What was the use of stepping out in faith, believing when You didn't back me up? My words and expectations were falling to the ground.

I developed a fear of stepping out and speaking the impossible because I didn't want to be disappointed again, and I didn't want to just look foolish for foolish sake. At least, if I looked foolish and You showed up, it would have been justified. It's a lonely enough life as it is without adding to it.

Now, You're asking me to believe again, step out again, trust You one more time for the impossible. Well, even if I didn't want to, my circumstances currently render me helpless otherwise. I have to believe for the impossible, and I have to trust You because no one else can rescue me from these depths, debts, deaths.

You know just how to get me to where You want me.

So, you're disappointed because things didn't go the way you wanted?

No Lord, it's not just that...what about the times when You were the one who asked me to step out or believe?
I felt like You didn't back me up.

If you had gotten it then, would your heart be where it is now?

No...

Do you understand that you're still alive and there's still time for those things to come to pass?

I suppose so...

There is nothing good that I will withhold from you once I know that your heart is for me, but I will do it at a time when it has maximum impact. My delay did not mean denial, besides, was I not the one who said it?

You have a point there.

Did it ever occur to you that I was wanting to far exceed your expectations? Where do you think you got that way about you- where you want to blow people's minds? I put that in you...You're just like me. I don't just want to surprise you; I want to blow your mind. There must never be a doubt in your mind or anyone else's that I did it. I'll come through for you, My Love.

SOME MONTHS LATER...

ANOTHER SITTING

It just occurred to me that we needed to have another heart to heart about this issue. As I begin to talk about this, I realise that it's an issue of trust. The thing is, I take You at Your word, and when I 'speak to my mountain' and believe, I do expect to have what I say. The 'how' is for You to decide, but I do expect it in a certain time also. To be honest, I must have been angry as well.

You say that You never change, and that You never lie. It didn't seem like this was true based on what I was seeing. The only reason why I've never left is because I know You. I don't understand everything You do, but I know that if You chose not to do something, You must have had a good reason because I know You love me.

We've been together for a while, and I know all Your thoughts concerning me are good. Your thoughts for me are much bigger and higher than I would ever imagine. You're not a set-up man. This is my consolation.

I said, "Yes," and I told You that You have free reign of my life, even if I'm kicking and screaming, snot running out my nose. I choose Your will, feelings aside. The thing is, I know I'll get over it. I always do.

No matter what happens, I love You, and I'll never leave You.

This is exactly the place I needed you to get to. Would your heart still be for me if I never did another thing for you? Would your heart be for me when things seemed to be contrary to my promises? Would you still praise me when things got rough? Does your heart pursue my heart, or does it pursue what you know I'm able to do for you?

How could there ever be any doubt in Your mind? We've come this far together. I didn't get here by myself.

Yes, and I know your heart is for me, but I wanted you to be certain of it. This is where our hearts become one, just as you've

asked. Just as I'd tested Abraham, so too, I've tested you, and you've come through as pure gold.
Now, I will pour out my glory on you. I can trust your heart towards my people.

I realise that in some twisted way, I'd made serving You about me and about results. I had connected my actions to an expectation of a corresponding action on Your part instead of remaining detached from the outcome.

Maybe..., but make no mistake, you came to me because you believed that I AM who I said I am and that I am a rewarder of those who diligently seek me. I am not mocked; you will reap what you sow. Don't be too hard on yourself. You have a tendency to do that. You judge yourself very harshly, when I don't condemn you.

UNLOCKING CHAMBER 3

Now, You're saying that it's ok to express whatever I feel and to come to You a thousand times to express my heart about the same issue. Even the unrighteous judge granted the persistent widow her request, how much more a loving Father? That's Your Word.

You are able to say anything to me, my beloved- even if you're expressing anger or disappointment. Whoever told you that I get tired of hearing you or tired of you coming to me? Who told you to ask once and leave it alone or that bringing it up again meant that you didn't have faith?
I AM concerned about your heart. Your emotions matter...

With me, you'll always have a safe space to be all of you. You will never be condemned, for I know you and I know your heart belongs to me...even when you're discouraged. I know all your thoughts and emotions anyway, but I desire to relieve you of your burden.

Somewhere along the way, I heard it said that God is not deaf and that He doesn't need me coming to Him all the time about the same thing. He knows already and if I have faith, I won't keep bringing it up. It came from the pulpit, and at the time, it made sense. I know now that this was not your heart. That thinking kept me burdened and bound.

UNLOCKING CHAMBER 4

At this juncture, You're telling me that I should open my heart, let go and stop taking on false responsibility for other's feelings to the point where I box myself in because of fear. Live, You said...

Live...

Well, that opened a whole can of worms for me. This amazing man came into my life after nine years of being single. I opened my heart to him, even though I knew that he was not my potential spouse. How could he be Your choice? After all, he's divorced (or is he really?).

When I thought I'd started to live, You said, *"Hold up, he's married. You can't go out with him, or it would make you an adulteress. Let not your good be spoken evil of. Take the high road, everyone gets protected."*

It is true Lord...and nothing should ever trump or compete with Your word in my life, but I need to let You know that I love him, I enjoy being in his presence, I care what happens to him, I love our conversations, I love how he makes me laugh, the stories he tells, the way he understands me, our connection, I love his maturity and his wisdom, I love his honesty and I love how he makes me feel…I love that he allows me to be me, and that he actually likes the little he knows of me, but still desires to know more.

I like the effortless way we interact, and I like that I'm safe to be me. I like that our purposes seem to align in the way they do…even though, I'm mindful of the fact that there are words spoken to me about Canada and migration that will potentially take us in opposite directions (the way things are now anyway).

I don't want to disrespect his wife or his family. I want to be above reproach, and I don't want to spoil my testimony. I'm terrified of making a wrong decision where marriage is concerned. By the way, how could my sister-friend dream that we got married? Who or what was the source of that dream?

Yet, I lay this all down for Your will Lord. Let me not ascribe any meaning or purpose to our relationship that You did not intend. You would not go against Your word, would You? Your word does not change… Have You not said that one is bound to one's wife or husband until death? Have I not lived this through with You? Let me not mess up all that You've done in me because of my emotions. Let me not mess up purpose or my testimony. May I remain pure and holy, acceptable unto You in the midst of what seems to be so much of what I desire and have desired for a long time.

In the past, these connections have never been Your will. How many Ishmael's will I have? I am totally confused as to why You would allow this relationship and have me to be working so closely with him and have him not be for me. My heart aches...but I suppose You trust me to do the right thing? I thank You for all that You're doing in my life in the midst of what I do not understand. I trust You...

Help me to manage my emotions in this scenario and to navigate according to Your will. May I learn the lessons You would have me to learn.

Someone says that I have to learn how to interact with men and still remain pure. He also said that I should lay my Isaac on the altar, even to the point of the knife coming down to kill him in the sacrifice. But this situation doesn't seem to fit that. Isaac was God's promise and God stopped Abraham from killing him. It feels more like there are so many reasons why he is not God's choice for me. So, he surely is another Ishmael, right? God would never give me another woman's husband. Divorced or not in the eyes of man, she's still alive, so he's still married in your eyes, Father.

Yet, there is a closeness, there is purpose for sure. If it were not for Your orchestration, we would not have been here having 'purpose conversations' now. I know our meeting was not by chance. I know that I'm supposed to be praying for him. We were destined to meet for sure.

I know most people won't understand the relationship that we have or even agree that it is truly YOU, but my main concern is that Your will be done, whatever the reason for it. At the very least, I've made a friend.

Voice in My Head: Has the Lord truly said, "You're bound to your spouse till death, and what does it truly mean to be reconciled to one's spouse?

Is anything you've thought or felt even real? Are you deceived? "These, the questions in my mind.

So, today I got that laying down of Isaac bit as it relates to the fulfillment of a purpose promise. Yes Lord, I lay it all down again. I can be a bit slow at times. Right now, I'm not even sure whether we are going forward with this project or not, all because I got distracted and mixed business with pleasure. Now, everything is muddled. I see the deliberate attempt to entrap in the spirit (or so I think)...yet, I know that all things will work together for my good, as long as I keep honouring you in purity.

UNLOCKING CHAMBER 5

I realise that I was very suspicious of my friend because of his beliefs and some of his associations. What started happening is that I started relating to him in fear and mistrust, thus going into self-protection mode. He may not have known that I was in self-defense mode, but I did and felt it in every fiber of my being.

Wouldn't the 'enemy of our souls' love to keep us both bound...me from sharing Your heart with him and him from hearing it.

You love everyone, and Your heart is not that any of us would perish.

Your love casts out all fear, and even if his intentions toward me weren't pure, the word says that I should

> *"Love your enemies, bless them that curse you, do good to them that hate you, and pray for them that despitefully use you and persecute you." Matthew 5:44*

So, I've decided to love... God's way... unafraid and unconditional. For love does not seek itself, and love believes all things. If he wasn't going to be a genuine friend to me, I was going to be one to him, as God would permit. I'm not a game player anyway, I don't have time or energy for that.

As I sit here in my emotional state, I write...

How many times must my heart break?
How many times must my dream die?
How many Ishmael's must come my way
Before I see your promises?

How much faith is enough?
It seems the target keeps moving.
I keep believing, though times are rough
But Lord, now I need to see things manifesting.

Birth through fire, death through fire,
Been trusting for my heart's desire.
It feels like it's not worth it
Yet, outside of you, there's no benefit.

How can I go deeper?
Seems like I don't know how anymore.
Where's the harvest for my seedtime?
When do I go through the open door?

UNLOCKING CHAMBER 6

"For we have not an High Priest who cannot be touched with the feeling of our infirmities; but was in all points tempted like as we are, yet without sin" Hebrews 4:15, KJV

My heart aches…
I can't speak…
For no words can be formed
To articulate this heart matter.
It feels like a broken heart that yearns to be caressed.
It feels like unrequited love…
It feels like mourning, and the irony of it is that
I'm the one who is dying.
What a sweet distraction it was…
A catalyst that has drawn me to this place
Where I now find myself.
Such a confusing time, this is, and
There are many questions, but the answer is ONE.
Oh, the sweet-bitter flavour of beauty
How it draws men to "Your heart,"
Yet, it leaves me with hope deferred,
As I hold the inner chambers open
That they may reach You.
Trusting my heart to You for the love that I desire.
How many times must I be down this road of loving-
Just for the sake of loving your way?
When will there be someone
Who holds an inner chamber open for me…
A safe place where You dwell?
Deep calls unto deep…
I thought there were no more chambers to open.
Seems, there was yet another 'untouched.'

I've been holding the view that You wouldn't want to hear me 'throw a pity party.' I'm thinking that if I cry out to You or share my emotions with you in this place, that it would be throwing a pity party. I've been told that You're not moved by this or that you're not interested.

But, shouldn't I be able to cry out to You, wherever I'm at, in whatever state I am? Isn't this what David did so often?

A voice nags, "Jilean, you need to suck it up and put on your big girl high heels." What do I do? Do I ignore or stifle my emotions? That can't be healthy. Actually, that seems a bit oppressive and dangerously explosive.

If my emotions have no outlet, and my tears don't flow, where do they go? Do I 'move on' by piling on other relationships and activities to cover over the rubble?

My emotions need to run their course without being rushed or judged, denied or ignored. They are most present. Let's deal with them.

I'm mourning the loss of a love...a love that I've desired for many years. I've waited and waited and even though I know that he is not Your choice given the obvious non-negotiables, our hearts are so entwined. I desperately need you to untangle us...

I can't remember the last time I cried like this. My very being knows that I need to let it all out. Yet, I'm having a mind battle about whether I can talk to You about all my thoughts and emotions. Should I articulate them or would I be throwing a pity party if I did? Will You see me as ungrateful or spoilt?

I figure, if I can't tell You everything and trust You with my heart, what's the point? Isn't that what intimacy is about? Don't You read my heart anyway? You know when something is troubling me. You know my thoughts, my desires, my fears and You love me anyway. You feel my heaviness, and You desire to be close. You desire to take it away and make everything better.

It seems that You've been desiring me to come higher for a while now, but I've been unsure just how to do that. Nothing I've tried seemed to have worked. So, You brought a 'sledge hammer' named Errol to utterly shatter the outer stoniness of my heart, so that You could perform surgery on the inner flesh. Ezekiel 36:26

I'm discovering that this process all begins with You. You allow whatever I need in my life to bring me to a place of brokenness. You break my heart to reach my heart and to mend it.

I'm thinking that this is what that dream two nights ago was about.

THE DREAM

I was graduating, and there was about to be a banquet in an upper level hall. I was at the bottom of the stairway to the hall. Someone I knew called out to me saying, "A priest is here looking for you."

I was thinking that I could not go upstairs 'looking like this,' and that I had to change my clothes first.

I didn't want to be seen the way I was. I had a sense that I knew him, but, "Surely, he could wait until I got upstairs, couldn't he? What was so important that it couldn't wait?"

I found myself hiding from him, and escaping to a dressing room, where I was trying to decide between two items of clothing.

THE INTERPRETATION

The priest represented You, Lord. How could I not have picked up on that while I was in the dream? In the dream, I was thinking about Esther and that I had to present myself as 'beautiful.'

As I pen the interpretation, I'm thinking, "How vain and prideful can you be Jilean?" Imagine, the Lord is requesting your presence, and you're hiding and thinking about what to wear? Cleanse my heart, Lord.

I see now that You wanted me to come to You as I am, in whatever state. You were trying to show me my heart condition and that I didn't need to feel like I needed to do anything before I came to You. You would embrace me just as I am.

Thank You so much. . . It's just like You to show me before I needed it. Now, that I'm here, I can reflect and, Your truth is unfolding. All is revealed in Your perfect timing.

Haven't I told you that I am close to the brokenhearted?
Psalm 34:18

Haven't I lived on the earth as you, my love? Do I not know this place of heartache and temptation? I know what it's like to have a broken heart and to love so deeply those who comprehended it not.

There is nothing you experience that I have not. It can seem like I live with a broken heart...think about how many people reject me every day. My love never sought itself.

Although, I willed to do the will of my Father, it was not without emotional turmoil. I would not have been able to endure to the cross had I not been in constant communication and intimate connection with Him, and still, I too have felt forsaken.

When you hurt, I feel it, and I want to make things better if you would open that part of your heart and allow me in. Even though I know, I want you to share everything with me...nothing is too big or too small. That brings us closer.

There's nothing you can't say to me. I love it when you share your heart with me...even when you don't have the words. I hear your heart's cry.

I understand, and I am well pleased with your sacrifice. There is nothing you'll ever do for me that won't be rewarded. Rejoice, for I will blow your mind with what I have in store for you.

TWO WEEKS LATER:

As I sat to talk with You about what I desired for us, I realised that this relationship with this man was a cheap substitute for what ours should be. It did help me to understand Your heart a bit better though. I also see how easy it is to be idolatrous by becoming totally consumed by an earthly relationship.

I understand now that two people can genuinely love each other, yet it becomes lustful when that relationship is not Your will for those two people, or even when things aren't in Your timing. We can be driving the vehicle in our own selfish desires, knowing that you've already said NO.

Your NO is a love word because it protects us from ourselves and from hurting others in the process. Your NO is never just about us, but about generations, just as Your Yes is.

You seem so unattainable at times. I'm journeying up, yet I never seem to reach You.

UNLOCKING CHAMBER 7

Just imagine, I've been staying away from Your presence because I didn't want it to seem as though I was only talking to You because I wanted You to do things for me. There have been so many things I wanted to talk about.

I've been carrying around burdens that You were more than willing to take, and I wasn't created to bear. I can't believe I've been guilt-tripping myself about this for so long.

Well, I guess you figured this one out on your own. You know that you can come boldly to me at any time. My arms are always outstretched, my ears always attentive. Nothing is hidden from me anyway. I know your heart toward me. I want you to Ask. It's my pleasure to do good things for my Beloved.

I'm learning that even 'Asking' is about posture before You. This too is a heart matter. Pride is what keeps us self-conscious, self-absorbed and separate.

So, I thought I would be flying in Your face if I talked to You about this matter again. I know what You have said. I need to obey.

I feel as though where this relationship is may constitute disobedience because we are so emotionally connected. In him, I've had a space to say whatever I was thinking or feeling.

He never said Jesus, but he has been so Jesus-like to me. So much more than those who claim to be Christians. This interaction has enabled me to see Your heart. I feel like defending him and covering him.

I have no clue what I'm doing anymore. My heart is breaking yet again. It feels as though I never get a break from a test, and the target keeps moving.

I'm frustrated from always trying to do the right thing.

How is it that you're back in this place again? I thought we dealt with this in Unlocking Chamber 1. You judge yourself and you think that I've judged you, when you'll always have a safe space to say or ask what you need to with me.

It's a good thing I never get tired of hearing you or seeing about everything that concerns you.

This is the space you need to create for the "Women Out the Box."

WHY HAVEN'T YOU ASKED?

Why haven't you asked?

My emotions don't matter to You, only obedience.

You're going back there?

Daddy, I love him.

If You had not said 'No,' our relationship would not have developed to the extent that it has. We have a level of intimacy I'd never thought possible with anyone.

So, what do I do with it now, and how do I open myself up to the possibility of another when he seems to be my dream come true? He's so much more than I thought I would ever get in one person. He didn't make my list, he surpassed it, except for three of my 'non-negotiables...'

The devil outdid himself with this one...so close and yet... As long as I remain in the center of Your will, You can bring about transformation for us both.

He's such an anomaly. How can he have the fruit of the spirit and not be Yours? It's baffling. I come across 'men of God' who are nowhere near him character wise. I'm irritated by the church that is supposed to be reaching out to those who don't know Christ.

Instead, we've expected people to come to the building, and we've judged them as we would 'the saved.' Who exactly is the church called to?

It seems we run in the opposite direction when we come into connection with those who don't know Christ, as though He who lives in us is not the Most-High God, greater than he who is in the world. We've been so fear motivated.

Why do we judge people by their past, as though we have none? I was not saved all my life and thanks to You, my past was never thrown in my face. You gave me hope for a better future. You allowed me to live my past down. Isn't this why Jesus came and why we are supposed to be sharing the gospel?

Not being able to proceed, abiding by Your 'No' gave me a most precious gift...that of fearlessness. It freed me to love without condition. I loved without thinking about getting hurt. I loved without wondering whether he was the 'ONE' because he couldn't be, right? I loved without fear.

If the restriction was to somehow disappear, I would be terrified. While everyone was so afraid for me because he was so wrong, and was saying, "Be careful," I had none of that because I had already surrendered to Your 'No.'

As far as religious folk are concerned, he is the last person one would expect God to choose for me. He does not fit the profile, yet inside of me there is a knowing of destiny. If he is for me, only You can change our current situation, and there is no man that can speak into the situation because Your word is clear.

THE MOST POWERFUL ANOINTING

Today, You sent a word or did You? It was prophesied that You've released me from the words of the past. They were sent to protect me from going down a disastrous and hurtful road. Some words are for a season and some words are for a lifetime.

I have heard You say though that now, You're doing 'a new thing.' You're wanting me to get rid of everything from the past…even my understanding of what You said. For You are wanting to pour new wine into me. As I get rid of the old, I will see the manifestation of many prophetic words springing forth. There will be an acceleration into destiny.

You said to me that I would be an adulteress if I saw him. Lord, it has been a difficult road given how I feel about him to honour Your word.

Yet, I have given this back to You over and over. I don't want to be deceived, and I genuinely want Your word to be fulfilled in his life and mine. If nothing ever comes of us, I want him to be Yours, and I don't ever want to get in Your way Lord.

We are both extremely thankful that You said, "No" initially because it allowed our relationship to develop into something so much deeper and more meaningful. I have no regrets, and if nothing ever comes of us, we will be great forever friends. Time has been our greatest ally, it allowed for deeper intimacy.

I can't fight this knowing in my heart that we are in each other's futures and that our destinies are intimately entwined. Since we've met, nothing but good has come out of it. These experiences have opened my eyes and heart to a truer picture of who You are and the way You love us.

Our relationship has birthed this book, and has given You entry into the chambers of my heart I didn't know were closed to You. For that, I'm forever grateful. I will never see You the way I used to again. Knowing You has freed me to love without fear.

Prophetic words have come forth in the past concerning every area of my life. The irony of it is that when these words began to unfold in a way that didn't fit the old mindsets and existing paradigms, the same people who delivered the word doubted God's work in my life.

My question is "How can a new thing look like an old thing? Can new wine fit into old wineskins?"

I've received many words about Esther in the past. Do we really understand that Esther was placed in the palace of a king who was not serving the God of Israel? Yet, God used her to turn the heart of the king and deliver her people from bondage. Esther married an 'unbeliever' in Christian terms, however he was open to the Lord because of Esther's heart.

I'm learning that Love truly is the greatest power in the universe. We can have every gift under the sun, and it would profit us nothing without love. Your love, Father never fails. Love does what gifts alone won't. I understand now why You've withheld me from flowing in certain gifts to develop a heart for your people. Love melts stony hearts. Love ensures that we keep You on the throne... front and center.

We can get deceived into thinking we're fine and powerful when we are operating in gifts. Love, Your Love is the most powerful anointing. Your heart is the greatest gift.

It does not judge or boast. It does not seek itself. Love gives without expectations. It gives regardless of the circumstances, regardless of the other's behaviour. Your perfect love gives no place to fear.

In fact, it casts out all fear. I chose to love this man Your way. Your saying 'No' allowed me to love him without fear, despite the things that I saw. The easier thing would have been to run. Now, I see a transformation in him in areas that would never have happened if I was seeking a change for myself.

Love causes us to do things we would not normally do. We subject ourselves to things we said and thought we would never do. Being Spirit led is a heart posture. We subject ourselves to the Lordship of Christ because of love...not what we want, but what He wants. This way is always best even though it hurts like crazy sometimes. After the rain, comes JOY.

I've learnt that we can't bring transformation to those we hold in contempt.

People are changed through relationship-relationship with God and then with others. When we build relationships, walls come down, ears hear and hearts become soft and pliable. Love is the one step approach to leading others to salvation. Love is truly the more excellent way.

If I had to summarise Christianity in one word, that one word would be LOVE. It's the reason why Jesus came, it is the summary of the 10 commandments, Love God with all your heart and love your neighbor as yourself.

It's the gospel or Good News. God so loved us that He gave Jesus. The Book of Revelation tells us that the testimony of Jesus Christ is the Spirit of Prophecy. By revelation, I now understand that Love is the Spirit of Prophecy, for God is Love, and though we prophecy and have not love, it is nothing.

The prophetic is about seeing people as God sees them and interacting with them on the basis of His love and who He created them to be and not condemning them for where they are NOW. It's about expressing His heart and extending His grace. I find myself now speaking to people as though they already are walking with the Lord and know it...

God sent Jesus because of love to walk out His love in the earth. We too are to walk as Jesus walked before the world. The prophetic is about becoming love and walking it out before the people as the signs and wonders that the earth groans to see.

THE NEW THING

Do not remember the former things, nor consider the things of old. Behold, I will do a new thing, now it shall spring forth; shall you not know it? I will even make a road in the wilderness and rivers in the desert. Isaiah 43:18-19 NKJV

God's doing a new thing right? But He's been doing it for a while now, and He's been trying to do more, but we are trying to fit that new thing into our old paradigms.

Instead of humbling ourselves and allowing Him to do what He wants, we rush off to put what He's said into our old boxes of operating and thinking. We think we KNOW already...

Or we think that we've heard wrong or it wasn't Him because it doesn't make sense in the context of our understanding.

So, we stifle our peculiarity because we think something's wrong with us. When, He created us the way He did ON PURPOSE. . . To do something different and NEW in the earth. If we're not willing to be different, God can't use us to do different.

Who is going to Break Out?

How come we talk love and faith, and we operate with each other in so much fear. . . As though there's someone or something higher or more powerful than the Highest God?

Perfect love casts out all fear. Love let's go and fear seeks to control.

And, God's Love NEVER fails...

Let's be careful not to knock what we do not understand just because we've never seen it before.

God is the one building His church, so shouldn't He be able to do it as He pleases? Who says it has to look or sound like anything we've been accustomed to?

Transition from the old to the new can be a very uncomfortable, unsettling, confusing place, and our tendency is to revert to what is familiar in order to maintain some semblance of control and normalcy.

It is in our weakness and instability that we tend to cry out to God more. In these moments, we should become more dependent, for it is in our weakness that He shows Himself strong. It is in these moments, we grow, and we KNOW Him more intimately.

Yet, not all of us weather this turbulence. We try to escape the discomfort and short-circuit the process that God has allowed to get us prepared for where He's called us to be.

Questions:

1. Why are we expecting the world to come to a church building?
2. Isn't the church supposed to go out into the world?
3. Why are we trying to get people to join a church instead of becoming the church/ kingdom citizens?

NOT ABOUT FEELINGS

Father, although I feel numb right now, I know that I love him.

Isn't this just like You Lord? There are times when I feel absolutely nothing, and nothing You're doing makes sense, yet still I love You and I know that You love me.

Being led by the Spirit of God is a heart posture. I do things that I wouldn't normally do for love. I 'subject' myself to the Lordship of Christ.

This is the place that You've called us to, one of surrender. Doing the 'right thing' doesn't always feel good, yet, Your peace is in the midst of it.

Besides, true love is about choosing not feeling...

EMBRACING MY PECULIARITY

For a long time, I struggled with my difference. It seemed more like a curse than a blessing…

There have been many seasons of aloneness, being misunderstood, questioning why I was the way that I am and wondering whether there was something wrong with me. "Why don't I think like everyone else?"

Now, I understand that my PECULIARITY is my super power. My peculiarity is a gift that will make room for me and bring me before great men and women. **I'm different because it's just how my Daddy made me.** I am the way I am because of what He created me to do.

Instead of asking "Why me?" I now count it a privilege to be chosen for all the things He has called me to.

Embracing my experiences and my differences has empowered me to walk out my purpose unapologetically. Peculiar is awesome!

I am God's Child, "Jill Out the Box."

JILL OUT THE BOX

I discovered my scribal gift when I was a teenager. Talking to my Dad was challenging for me, and I started writing as a means to vent emotionally because I felt like I couldn't talk to him. My thoughts flowed very easily when I wrote, and I found writing to be very cathartic. One thing that has always happened when I write is that God expresses His heart.

Eventually, I started writing poetry. One day, I took some of my writings to school and showed my friend. She said, "These are quite good. You should share them or publish them." I tried sending them to various newspapers to no avail. Then, I sent them to card companies and explored the possibility of becoming one of their writers.

I received one response which said that they already had in-house writers and don't take unsolicited work. Then, one day it dawned on me, "Jilean, why are you trying to have other people publish your cards when you can have a card company of your own?" Many years would pass, but not without there being a full-blown dream in my heart. Sometimes, the dream God placed in our hearts will only make sense to us...

Over the years, I put myself out there, and people actually paid me to do personalised cards and verses for them as gifts for their loved ones. One fateful day, as I was walking through the mall, I stumbled upon this ceramic picture frame that I thought was full of character. I bought it and took it home...immediately, I was inspired to write something to put inside of it. I took this to work to show another friend of mine and she said, "Jilean, you should sell these."

So started the sale of frames with verses. These always sold themselves. People never needed any persuasion. This went on for as long as I kept getting interesting frames to buy at a reasonable price.

When I got married to my first husband, I registered Jill Out the Box Ltd. as a card and written expression company. The process for coming up with the name went something like this, "Jack and Jill went up a hill, Jack in the Box, Jill out the Box. Hmm, I love that, Jill Out the Box it is." At the time, I had no idea just how loaded that name was in terms of who I am and my calling. Loaded as it was, there were those who would laugh when I said it.

Post-divorce, it became JOTBox Ltd. (Story in JOTBox Is Alive chapter) and the Lord said to me that it's a publishing company.

I didn't know the first thing about publishing, but if God said it, I believed Him, but had no idea how He was going to bring that to pass. I rested in the fact that God doesn't call the equipped, but He equips the called. I purchased this book on starting a self-publishing company, and to my surprise, many of the things they were saying I should do, I had already done.

To date, one of my Letters to the Editor was published in the newspaper, as well as an interview in my capacity as a Life Coach. I've written pieces for two publications and co-edited for one. More recently, I've had the opportunity to read some of my work at 'Reading Under the Trees,' an opportunity I initially got because a friend had asked me to write her something for the 25th Anniversary of an Adult Literacy organisation.

I'm not the person who always excelled in Literature or Language at school, and I'm not a big reader. I don't have any literary awards or accolades. Writing just comes naturally to me, and I'm able to connect with people's hearts and express what's hard for them to express in writing. It is a gift from God, and as His word says, *"A man's gift makes room for him and brings him before great men."* Proverbs 18:16

I can attest that using my gifts and pursuing my purpose have indeed brought me before great people. In fact, I'm now married to one of them. If I hadn't been using what God gave me, I may not have met Errol. My written expression spilled over onto God Powered T-shirts for which Errol later became Brand Ambassador.

God has placed in every one of us a gift or gift mix that can propel us to ***greatness*** and cause us to prosper when we entrust them to Him and give Him charge of our lives. In us are solutions to problems in the world. Besides, if we don't use what He has given us, we will lose it.

Deuteronomy 8:18 says, *"But you shall remember the Lord, thy God: for it is He who has given you the power to get wealth that He may establish His covenant which He swore unto your fathers..."*

I've said all of this to say, follow that gift or those dreams that God has placed in your heart, for He created us with His purpose in mind. It is in living our purpose that we find fulfilment. He wants even more than we do to bring about the manifestation of our 'dreams' for His name's sake. He says in Jeremiah 29:11 *"For I know the thoughts that I think toward you, thoughts of peace and not of evil, to give you an expected end."*

Here are some other clues as to where your purpose might lie:

1-Things you love to do

2- Things that others say you do well

3- The thing in the world that really upsets you

4-The things that won't leave you alone

5-The thing you struggled with most or that caused You the most pain

6-The things you saw in your dreams (when you're asleep, but also what you daydream about often)

7-A traumatic or life changing event

8- The things you would still do for free and pour your energy and finances behind.

Purpose is not a destination but a journey...

We often talk about walking in our purpose as though it is a singular thing that we are called to do. That can be confusing if you're still searching for what that one thing is. **It's more about alignment than assignment, and getting on a path than getting to a place.**

Getting fixated on purpose being 'one thing' may cause us to be limited in how we are able to be used. The key is being willing and available to the Master.

In actuality, there may be many things that we do when we are walking in purpose. Those things may even be different at different points in time.

In my experience, the key is starting with a question to our loving Creator, and walking our lives out in relationship with Him, one step at a time. Things unfold as we go along in willingness to follow His lead.

There's no limit to what we can do with Him. It's a process of Loving, Letting Go and Listening. Loving God and knowing that we are loved, letting go of our preconceived notions, old mindsets, offenses, wrong relationships, and being open to hear what He tells us in the innumerable ways He does, and finally, following His lead.

GOD POWERED

Four years ago, the Lord woke me up with a verse, "Not by might or power, but by my Spirit." Minutes later, the design was downloaded...This was the answer to a dream to do T-shirts on a larger scale.

I got favour, and the graphic was done for me free of charge. Months later, He said to me to step out, print and launch. The scripture was about how Isaac sowed in a famine and reaped hundredfold in the same year. I printed over 100 Tees, and I broke even in three weeks. God is faithful.

Today, the God Powered brand has a presence in at least 17 countries, including the Caribbean, Central America, the U. S. A., Canada and the United Kingdom. I would not have imagined. It blew my mind that people not only connected with the message, but wanted to make a statement by wearing the tee, buying them as gifts, owning more than one color and dressing their families. God is extravagant.

He just showed off when He gave me a then Brand Ambassador turned husband... All from passionately pursuing purpose. For me, the brand is more than just a design. It's a message, a movement and a lifeline. I could not have done it in my strength. It was only by the grace and power of Almighty God... And we've only just begun. We're ramping up a God Powered Revolution.

REVOLUTION

We're starting a revolution
A GOD POWERED REVOLUTION.
Things can't stay the same-
They must change by the power of His name.
Turning the town upside down
Transition to a place I've never known
So confusing, yet amazing
New thoughts, new dreams, New ME.
Different we are, healed, yet scarred
Embracing who we truly are
Created to be peculiar
A chosen generation
Born to start a revolution.
My peculiar is powerful
My scars make me beautiful
Sticking out, not blending in
Transforming from His gift within
I was born to start a REVOLUTION.
Ever evolving, ever resolving
Ever Being, ever creating, ever Loving…
REVOLUTION!!!

**God Powered Revolution is available in a T-Shirt*

JOTBOX IS ALIVE!!!

I used to have a company called Jill Out the Box Ltd. After my divorce, I regrettably had to dissolve it. Consequently, I was in a position where I had to find a new name and re-register the company. The name Jill Out the Box was a very loaded one which I knew the Lord had given me and to me, nothing else measured up.

I came up with the name Liberate Inc. which turned out to be taken in every possible variation. Prior to finding this out though, something strange began to happen...

I started receiving baffling e-mails on my phone. Picture this scenario, you're on your computer composing an e-mail to someone, and in the middle of that, you get an e-mail from yourself dated some years before. It's was not a forward.

The timing of it was so incredible because at the time of that email, I was having the ideas for the company, and I had sent myself the e-mail to document and remind myself. In this e-mail, I had shortened the name of the company for ease in writing. The phenomenon of the e-mails went on for about 2 days. I even got one that was blank- no sender, no subject. I was convinced that it was God, so I decided to write back to jehovah@god.com. To my wonder and amazement, the e-mail never bounced...it went Lord knows where.

On the day I found out that Liberate Inc. was taken, I asked God, "What now?" and His answer was another e-mail. For the first time, I saw that the new name was staring me straight in the face all along...JOTBox (Jill Out the Box). Not only is 'JOT' an acronym, but it is a play on words. Only God could have done that, I'm not so clever. It means to write down, or to leave a mark, but it also means to stick out. What a loaded name indeed? It certainly was now more meaningful than it had ever been, given that it is a written expression/publishing company.

Believe you me, I know just how all this sounds, but I will make myself a fool for the glory of God any day- even if I have to stand alone and face persecution. I would not be where I am today were it not for His love.

I applied for JOTBox and was refused. I was devastated. I was so certain that because of 'all the strange' that for sure God wanted me to use this name. "How could He set me up like that," I thought. At that time, He said to me that in order for this business to be successful in Him, it had to first die, and that if I still believed, it would be mine. It died to live that His name might be glorified. (Reference John 11 and 12, the story of Lazarus)

I can't remember how long after my first blank it was, but one morning, I picked up my bible at the side of the bed, and it was on the same scripture that the Lord had given me concerning this situation back then. I was so grateful and confident about this because it was as though He was confirming His word to me and letting me know that He was going with me.

Today, I am here to testify that God is GREAT and FAITHFUL. He is so real and so personal, and He will do what He says He will do as long as we trust Him- no matter how things look. After dying a death, that name has risen, just as Jesus Christ did, just like Lazarus did by His power. JOTBox is alive!!!

I applied again after putting some things in order that God had spoken to me about. One of them was using my savings to pay off my debt. The debt was all gone, hallelujah, but trust me when I tell you, I had to have heard from Him to do that because I really couldn't see where my money was going to come from. When I went to collect the application results, the name was approved. JOTBox rose again. Of course, I had already by faith gone ahead and secured the domain name on My Father's instruction. How cool is He?

God doesn't change. The same things He did back then are the same things He can and will do now, if we would only take Him at His word. He has and always will be a God of the Impossible. Jesus came, He died for us and rose again, and so can every situation in our lives if we only believe.

DESTINY COACH

I've always been a people-person, and I love to travel. When I was choosing my course of study, I wanted to do Hotel Management & Tourism or Public Relations. It turns out that I had to do a degree that was offered at the school that I had to go to because it was close to where my aunt lived in Halifax.

That degree was Human Resource Management & Industrial Relations. It was still people-related, so I did not mind. I felt that HR would permit me to make a difference in the lives of people. I figured that if people were going to spend so much of their lives at work, they should at least enjoy what they did.

As it turns out, having done HR, I worked at two hotels and an airline. I was still able to dabble in Marketing and Public Relations, and I've done a bit of travelling. I still got to do the things I wanted to despite the degree I did. ***(Nothing is wasted with God. He won't let what He placed in us go to waste.)*** I still had that desire to help people on a more personal level though, but corporate HR did not function quite the way I had imagined.

When I lived in Barbados, I had the opportunity to work with a friend of mine who was a Life Coach. That was the first time that I'd heard about Coaching, and I never thought at the time that I'd become a Coach.

It would be years and much life drama later before it occurred to me that people were always telling me their personal business. I would be minding my own business, and they'd start talking to me about the intimate details of their lives. I said, "God there must be a way to do this and get paid for it." Coaching found me, and the doors opened for me to be able to do a certification with an academy in Australia.

I thoroughly enjoyed that journey, and felt that I had made the right choice not doing an MBA. You see, when I worked at the Management Consulting firm, an MBA was the thing professionals were doing to be able to command higher salaries.

I never had a desire to do one because I felt it was too much reading and I would probably waste a lot of money and never finish it. There was no passion or excitement, and money was not a motivator for me. At one point, I thought that maybe I was not ambitious or something was wrong with me. I realise that the same thing I wanted for others is what I wanted for myself. I wanted to love what I do, and I knew myself enough to know that an MBA was not for me.

How many more people are out there thinking that they are unambitious or lazy because they just haven't found what motivates them? How many people are in jobs that they're not wired to do?

Coaching came naturally to me, and in true God modus operandi, He had already begun to prepare me for it through Women Out the Box, church and life experiences. We had to start an online blog or journal at the beginning of the programme and maintain it throughout. I was already posting regularly in WOTB.

The thing I loved most about Coaching is that I didn't need to know the answers because the client already did. It is an empowering tool that renders the coach less and less needed. It is an approach that reduces the risk of witchcraft and manipulation because the client has to do the work and make his/her own choices.

Every person's purpose is as unique as his/her finger print. Likewise, every person's path is unique. This is why we need to have a relationship with God to be guided on the path that is right for us. As a Coach, I help people to become aware of His presence and guidance in their lives.

Most times, following 'Steps to Success' won't work because they weren't personal or specific to the individual. For continuation on a purpose path, there must be buy in or a vested interest. The direction should come from within and not without.

A coach helps create awareness for clients to find the answers that are right for them and provides the desired support to help them achieve their goals.

I'd always hear pastors saying that we should find our purpose, but no one seemed to be able to say how we should do that. So, I asked God and He took me on a journey to discovering what He created me to do. I'm still journeying, but I'm on the right path for me.

I've found that the simplicity in knowing what we're created to do is in first knowing the One who created us. The more we develop our love relationship with Him is the more we know ourselves and receive guidance for our lives.

It is my joy and privilege to help others find that fulfillment that comes from walking out destiny.

How We Got Here

WHERE IT ALL BEGAN

This is the story of how I came to this place of having these chambers of my heart locked.

We met at work and were courting for under a year before he accepted a job in another Caribbean island. On December 14th 2002, we were married at home, and then I migrated to join him there.

He was very different from anyone I'd ever met… and he treated me well prior to our marriage. One thing that stood out to me was his thoughtfulness.

I thought we were on the same page as far as relationship with God was concerned…

On my honeymoon, I discovered where he went and what he did on his bachelor's night out. But, that wasn't the thing that caused the tears, it was how he spoke to me and his response to my asking some questions. Based on who I believed him to be, I was pretty surprised and disappointed about the choice. I thought to myself, "Who did you marry and what have you done?"

In January 2003, I stumbled upon a letter written to my husband which suggested a relationship he was having unbeknown to me prior to our marriage. Meaning, while he was engaged to me, he was having relations with this person.

What a start, right?!!

In a way, I think my marriage was doomed to fail (although this is not the truth) because I felt like I wasn't given all the information to make a more informed decision. Certain facts were intentionally hidden from me.

I also felt in the marriage like it was cruel to start me at zero given that he had 'feelings' for this other person prior. Why would someone do that to anyone? He was seeing her before we got married, so he didn't need to marry me. Then, to make matters worse, that relationship was never severed completely when we were married. Did our marriage ever have a fair chance?

There was a point before marriage when we broke up, and it probably should have remained that way. When I asked directly whether there was someone else in the picture, I was told "No, I'm just scared because I've failed at marriage before." At the time, it seemed plausible, and I chose to believe him.

Nothing really prepared me for marriage… And you don't know you're not whole until you are.

I truly loved my husband, but I loved him in the only way I could have (at that time). I couldn't give what I didn't have, and I would say the same for him.

There was a time when I wanted to view him as the monster and myself as the victim. It was easier to cast blame and not accept any personal responsibility for the way things went down. There are no monsters, only hurt /imperfect human beings.

Truth is, I made him responsible for my happiness and completeness, and that's a very heavy burden for anyone to carry. That's why it's God's job, with my agreement and partnership of course.

I will say this: I could have been the best wife in the world, he still made a choice to be unfaithful. It wasn't because I was undesirable, it wasn't because of any number of reasons that I could list here… It was his choice. That's not on me. ***Please stop blaming yourself for other people's choices. It's a burden you weren't meant to carry.***

He also made me responsible for filling his void and making him happy. It's something we humans tend to do…

Did I cause him to be manipulative, emotionally abusive? I think in some way, I permitted it, and I did so for fear of rejection and fear of "What would I do if he leaves…?" I didn't realise that what we try to hold on to in fear, we lose anyway. I didn't KNOW then that only God is my source, so I permitted many things through neediness.

I'm often asked, didn't you see the warning signs?

Yes, and No… *If* only I knew then what I know now. Hindsight is 20/20 vision.

When he kept asking me, "How do you know that I'm the one for you?" RED FLAG!

When he said, "I'm just scared because I have had one failed marriage." RED FLAG!!!

Marriage should NEVER be entered into unless you both have the peace of God because when the going gets tough, you should both know that it was God orchestrated, and that He is the one who is going to see you through and keep you together.

It is ill advised to enter into marriage with emotional baggage or a fear of failure from past relationships. This means that there must be a deep healing and restoration to wholeness before considering a life-long covenant.

Post-divorce, I determined that entering into a relationship with a divorced man is a non-negotiable for me (unless his wife is dead). (I now have to say 'was' a non-negotiable, but God…) I will explain my reasons why in the chapter called "Why God Hates Divorce."

I can't say that I was treated badly before, or that he spoke to me *in a disrespectful manner*. In fact, I was treated quite well.

I believe that there are some things that only show their heads when the right conditions arise… i.e. marriage.

WHAT MY MARRIAGE WAS LIKE

One of the things I never aspired to have was a marriage like that of my parents. Yet, despite my best efforts, I woke up one day and realised that it was the very thing that happened. In fact, in some respects, it was worse. Let me say though that I've watched God do an awesome transformation over the years in their marriage, and there is so much I see now in their marriage that I do desire in my own. I admire many beautiful things, and I see a strength now in what I thought was weakness. I see longevity, perseverance, unconditional love. The possibility exists as well that I was unable to see the 'good things' before.

When we look at people and situations through the glasses of fear and pain, we miss the beauty and virtue in them.

I was living out the role of my mother, and he assumed the role of my father. In actuality, it was more of a parent-child relationship than one of two equal adults. It is said that the very things we fear come upon us.

My desire and vision for a marriage was based on what I saw and didn't want rather than a healthy, God-defined vision. Also, I didn't understand submission and unconditional love then in the way I do now. Without being healed and breaking free from those chains of my past, I was set to live out what I saw, even though I knew in my mind that I wanted something different.

We also attract who we are and not who we desire, so the best way to attract who and what we desire is to become. When the enemy of our soul comes and finds no strong place to hold on to, he can't attach himself.

I felt as though I could do nothing right. It's hard to adequately describe what emotional abuse is like to someone who has not experienced it. It can tend to sound like you're complaining. Because I had lost count of how many times I'd heard, "Marriage is hard work," I'd come to believe and accept that what I was experiencing was the 'hard.'

For a long time, I'd thought that what I was experiencing was 'normal,' even though it didn't feel right at all. I believe that most of us know when we've been touched by the love of God, and this was not that.

I was regularly told that I didn't understand what marriage was really like because I hadn't been married before, and that he had experience. I would be accused of being 'just like his previous wife,' though we were very different people. Many of the things he would say to me about me, it would appear he was looking in a mirror.

I never knew what the right thing to say was. I was constantly walking on eggshells. I doubted myself in the simplest of decisions. Any praise I had gotten would be shattered and cancelled out soon thereafter. I was expected to assert myself as a wife, yet whatever I said or felt was invalidated ("Behave yourself" or "Don't feel that way"). I lived on an emotional roller coaster, up today, down tomorrow, and I felt like a basket case.

It seemed to me at the time that my husband seldom accepted wrong or responsibility for anything. Any 'apology' would sound like, "I'm sorry you felt that way," but never, "I was wrong, I apologise for saying or doing..." After all, he was only doing it for my own good, and I shouldn't be 'so sensitive.'

It felt like I was living with two completely different people. When Mr. Charming was around, he'd never remember what 'The Stranger' said. On the outside, Mr. Charming was well respected, and people knew how great Jilean was. However, Jilean seldom heard all those things at home, or would be cut down to size very soon after being told. Let me say here that it's not that we didn't have 'good times,' but given what happened outside of those, it's as though they were overshadowed by the painful times.

Important issues never got dealt with in any great detail or were not resolved. The focus seemed to be on moving on, as there was an inability or unwillingness to deal with anything emotional. As a result, they kept coming up on my part, and he'd say to me that I was 'always bringing up the past.'

Often, decisions would be made unilaterally on his part after we'd had an in-depth discussion and come to an agreement. As a result, I stopped putting forward my views in any forceful way because I felt that they weren't going to be considered anyway, and we'd be doing what he wanted. I was just being asked by him as a formality; so, it could be said that I had been asked. Sadly, many of these decisions adversely impacted our family life, and I was expected to wholeheartedly support them.

What seemed to be a minor difference of opinion too often escalated into a 'big thing,' ending with a comment like, "If you want to leave, then leave." I'd be left wondering, "How did we get here?" The effect of this is I'd be afraid to raise issues, and there was a feeling of instability and insecurity. I feared he'd leave me.

At that time, my identity, confidence and trust in God as my Source were not solidified to the extent that I knew I'd be fine if he had left me. I realise that I was too dependent on him for my happiness, my identity, my direction and my provision, and I'd made him my god and idol. I know now that my love tank was not full and in some way, I was expecting from him what no one but God could give me.

There were times when I felt like he was talking to someone who was telling him negative things about me or trying to turn him against me. I would say, "I am not your enemy, I'm for you." It would feel as though I was being attacked, and I was spoken to with such contempt. When we were physically intimate, it would feel as though there was a block between us.

After a disagreement, any suggestion that we should pray about things would be met with, "I can't pray with you, we have a different spirit." Now, I see that he was actually telling me the truth. At several points in my marriage, I asked myself, "If he really loves me, how could he treat me this way? And if he really loves God, how could he treat me this way?"

As a wife, this cut to my core. He often used his words as a sword that pierced my heart. When there are no bruises on the outside, people seem to think that you can stay and work it out, but emotional abuse is a slow, steady and too often silent killer. It kills dreams, it kills purpose, and it can kill physically as well.

In order for it to be dealt with, it needs to be exposed. **Evil thrives in darkness and secrecy.**

What made things worse was his mindset that "I don't want people in my business." So, there was an unwillingness to get counselling or help. This spelt isolation for me.

On this note, before any help could be sought, I needed to 'wake up' to the reality of the situation, and not just be deluded into thinking that every couple has problems. There are problems, and there are PROBLEMS!

I had two awakenings, I'm uncertain as to the order in which they came. Awakening one, I was in an emotionally abusive relationship. The second was staring me in the face all along…my husband was unsaved.

The word says that, we know them by their fruit. (Matthew 7:20/John 13:35) In a real-world vernacular, it would be said like this: "If it looks like a duck and walks like a duck, then by golly, it's a duck."

Sometimes, we make excuses for people's behaviour because we have made an inaccurate assessment of who they really are, or we are afraid to face the reality of our situation.

With my eyes wide open, I was faced with another dilemma…Who do you go to? It's certainly not about people with titles and designations.

There are pastors and professionals who won't be able to provide the right kind of assistance for the emotionally abused. Spirituality alone won't help, and there are practical things that need to be done. Make no mistake, there is a spiritual component behind all forms of abuse. I will not go into that here.

However, praying about it and trusting God alone won't help if nothing is done differently. There must be a separation of some sort, even if it's only emotional in order to protect the 'victim.' It may not always be a physical separation, as it relates to cohabitation, but it must happen. It is a matter of sanity and preservation. During this separation, both parties must allow for a deep, healing work on their hearts before there can be any reconciliation.

In the final analysis, it is a heart matter, and it didn't start in marriage, but began way before then. Just as in the natural, plaque can build up around our hearts, so too in the spiritual, the issues of life can cause our hearts to harden and become stony.

Heart disease due to a build-up up of plaque in the valve prevents blood flow to the heart. Life is in the Blood.

MOVEMENTS AND PROJECTS

What I didn't tell you was that when we moved back to Trinidad, we lived in a rented house in the east with relatives for a while. They eventually moved into their new home, leaving us there for some time after. We were renovating a house two streets away, and at the same time, the dream house was being built. As if our marriage needed any more stress! But there always needed to be a project or two going on.

This served a dual purpose, I think; for him to avoid intimacy and spending time with me, and to feed his ego. In his mind though, he was doing it all for his family.

He started doing CFA the year our son was conceived, (despite agreeing that he would not have started then) and that took up most of his 'us' time when he wasn't working.

Prior to living in the east, there was a period of time where he was renting an apartment 'to study' and our son and I lived at my Mom's in south Trinidad. It was as though he had the luxury of pretending he didn't have a family until it was convenient. I would be accused of being selfish and insensitive if I made any request of him because I should have understood that he had **his studying** to do.

We eventually moved into the renovated house on our anniversary in December 2008, our son was nearly three (he had not come home the night before, and he never called. I assumed he had slept at the 'Reno' because he had been staying there most of the time as soon as it was possible to 'get some studying done').

I was putting his stuff in what I thought was our master bedroom, when he said, "It's okay, you stay in that room, and I'll stay in this one." In effect, we had separated that night, although it wasn't stated officially then. I can't tell you why I complied with tears in my eyes, but that night was the last we would 'make love.' I cried because it felt like my marriage was over…sort of like when someone dies. I mourned the loss of my husband long before he actually died.

MARRIAGE AIN'T FOR BABIES

Marriage is not for babies, 'spoilt children' and half people. It's for grown-ups.

Sad part is we can look grown up and not be mature. I realise that this was the case with me, but I only knew when I knew. In hindsight, we were two incomplete, emotionally and spiritually immature people trying to become complete off each other.

I've tried one too many times to fill up on 'empty' and placed God in a box where He was not accessible to me.

LOVE LET'S GO AND FEAR HOLDS ON...

God doesn't force us to love Him and He loves us despite our flaws and wicked ways. We can't do anything to earn His love, He just does. . . And He has given us free will- the ability to choose, and by extension, the ability to break His heart.

So, why do we try to force and manipulate others?

No one wants to feel as though he or she is not enough. . . And I don't ever want to feel as though I have to beg or connive for someone's affections.

Truth:

WE CANNOT GIVE WHAT WE DO NOT HAVE

Each person in a relationship brings value, and that value is often in the 'differences.' Those differences are connected to purpose and the unit being balanced and purposefully functional and effective. If we don't know our value, we won't be able to appreciate that value in others.

We are often trying to change in others the thing that God intended to use to bless us and to bring depth and increased value to our lives if we could only submit to Him.

When we know our *Source of everything,* we won't be holding on to anything or anyone for dear life out of fear. Most times, we get this revelation in the deepest struggles of our lives, in the 'impossible' situations, or in the thing that feels as though it was meant to destroy us.

That's when we cry out because there's nothing we can do to save ourselves, and 'The God of the Impossible,' the 'I AM' everything that we need shows up.

He is strongest to us in our moments of weakness.

"Concerning this thing I pleaded with the Lord three times that it might depart from me. And He said to me, "My grace is sufficient for you, for My strength is made perfect in weakness."" II Corinthians 12:8-9

PRAYING FOR MARRIAGES... NOT

I never pray for marriages, but for individuals, as I've learnt that marriage is not an entity unto itself, but rather the 'becoming one' of two whole individuals who are intentional about their relationship and committed to an expected outcome. My prayers are for persons to see themselves the way God sees them, to know that they are loved, to be healed of their pain and to come into right relationship with Him.

Marriage is a choosing, although so many operate on auto pilot or are brain dead. Marriage is a way of relating, it's about each individual having a mind that is fully persuaded. Can two walk together, except they agree?

If the two individuals in question do not desire the same outcome, aren't guided by the same principles, or one or both parties are unwilling to compromise or self-sacrifice, then the relationship will 'not work.'

It seems, we put so much effort into our jobs or careers, sports, even maintaining our vehicles, but marriages are just expected to work. A relationship, any relationship, at some point takes effort to be harmonious. There must be an agreed upon context or basis that guides it and directs focus on matters of priority.

Many of us go into marriage for self-*ish* reasons. One popular one is "I just want to be happy."

NEWSFLASH:

If we aren't happy by our lonesome, we won't we happy in marriage.

Marriage is about giving much more than it is about taking. It is meant to be complementary and not supplementary.

If you lack love, my love won't fill you. If you don't already come with your love tank full, you certainly won't be able to give selflessly to your spouse without feeling cheated, inadequate or resentful. In a marriage relationship, both spouses should be giving to the other what is needed and not seeking to get what each needs. This void can only be filled by Father's love (God's Agape love).

Post-divorce, the Lord would say to me, "Pray for him," to which I retorted, "What can I pray for him that I haven't prayed for already?" Believe me when I tell you that's the last thing I wanted to do, but **Daddy** always wins...so, I prayed.

One of the things that happened is that my prayers began to change. I wasn't praying for my marriage or my husband because that was already done as far as I was concerned. I no longer had any hopes or expectations of him 'making me happy.'

Side Note:

I don't think anything can fully prepare us for marriage. Some things are learnt in the living. There has been a practice in the church of Pre-marital Counselling. I'm not saying that it should not be done, however it is my belief that the way it is done has not been effective.

What usually happens is that the couple, once they get to the stage where they desire to be married, would speak to the pastor and enroll or be enrolled for Marriage Counselling sessions, often for a specified length of time or number of sessions.

My issue with it is whether two people are well suited or not, emotionally healthy or not, these pre-marital sessions are a formality...a thing to do before getting married. Often times, date is set, dress is already bought and wedding planned prior to the commencement of these sessions. Regardless of the discoveries or arising issues, most of the couples are still going to get married. I don't need to tell you about the divorce rate these days, do I?

What I propose is Wholeness Counselling for individuals who are interested in one day becoming married prior to them meeting their potential spouse. This allows for a more authentic picture of individuals and a 'no-pressure' space for self-discovery and sound counsel without deadlines.

I figure that I can't say things like this and not walk my talk. Even though I felt as though God had taken me through a process of healing and deliverance post-divorce, I submitted myself to a counselling session (with a well- established, professional, Family Life and Marriage Counsellor) to assess my spiritual and emotional preparedness for marriage. I did it in my singleness with no potential spouse in sight.

Our session dug deep, but at the end of it, I had a clean bill of health. In her words, "You're good to go." There was no cause for concern, and she didn't feel the need for us to have any follow up sessions at that time. According to her, it's not that we don't enter into marriage with issues to work out, but it's more about how we approach dealing with our issues, for none of us are perfect.

She's one of two people I highly recommend. One of the reasons is I know her husband as well, and I know the kind of marriage they enjoy. A word to the wise is sufficient.

LEAVE WITHOUT LEAVING

Is it possible to leave a marriage without physically leaving? Yes, people do it all the time when they checkout emotionally.

They stay married, they live in the same space, they share food and child-rearing responsibilities, but as far as relationship and intimacy go, they're absent. In effect, it's like having an unspoken separation or living with a room-mate depending on the level of 'distance.'

For many couples, this is the reality they live and they've gotten used to it. It has become a sort of 'normal' and they've stopped giving thought to it.

For some, it is a painful space for one or both parties because they deeply desire to connect and don't know how. For others, it's easier to not deal with the pain of betrayal or whatever is causing the distance. Yet, others have emotional affairs or inappropriate external relations to fill the void they feel.

In my case, where there was emotional abuse, leaving without leaving became a necessity in order to preserve my sanity and health.

I shared earlier that I made my husband responsible for my happiness. My emotions were entirely wrapped up in him. When he was happy, I was happy and when he wasn't, well, I certainly wasn't. As a result, I lived on an emotional roller coaster because I gave my power to him. I made him my god. In a sense, I allowed him to validate who I was...which was never good enough.

There came a point when my whole world crumbled, and I realised that no matter what I did, the situation was not changing. He was not giving up the outside relationship, nor was he about to come clean about it.

In my mind, there was nothing left to salvage, and there was nothing that I did not try. We were going through a separation, but we were living in the same space, for logistical, financial and child-sensitive reasons.

In order to cope, I had to take myself out of the relationship emotionally. What this meant was that I looked to God to satisfy my need for love and affirmation, and I relinquished all expectations of my 'room-mate' of a husband.

I was civil and continued to cook and do all the things I normally would (with him opting not to eat from me for a time and also telling me that I didn't need to wash his clothes). Yippee right?

It was painful on some level because I couldn't believe that he would not eat from me. On reflection, 'When one has cocoa in the sun drying, he has to watch for rain.' It was never in my heart or mind to do him harm.

Correction, I didn't do ALL the things, and I'm not going to try to justify or prove scripturally whether it was right or wrong. This was a personal decision.

I decided that if I wasn't going to be the wife, then "I wasn't going to be the whore." Plain talk. I decided that I was not going to play Russian roulette with my life, already having to deal with recurring infections.

In addition, I felt that the marriage covenant had been broken with no remorse, admission or intention to mend the breach. The dynamic was not one of honesty, trust or intimacy, but purely one where I was expected to pretend that all was well and render my body for his physical gratification.

The irony of this is that he tried to justify his distance by saying that I was rejecting him, when this only occurred after his unwillingness to treat with the 'elephant in the room.'

I heard a male say recently that this move on my part is actually what most women do and that it is actually perceived as rejection. He implied that I should have continued to be intimate with my husband, especially if I knew he was with someone else. At the time of this conversation, I was totally opposed. Read on...

This is what the word says about this matter:

I Corinthians 7:4

> *The wife's does not have authority over her own body, but yields it to her husband. In the same way, the husband does not have authority over his own body, but yields it to his wife.*
>
> *Do not deprive one another except with consent for a time that you may give yourselves to fasting and prayer; and come together again so that Satan does not tempt you because of your lack of self-control.*

In my understanding, this is said in the context of covenant and does not apply to a scenario where that covenant has been broken. However, the word does not give any such detail, but offers one exception, mutual agreement.

Permit me to go down a perilous road here for a minute. If we believe that soul ties are formed through sex and this is a way that spirits are transferred, wouldn't it also hold true that the 'sex' that created the bond with the 'outside woman' would allow the anointing to be transferred through the wife and break the yokes of bondage? If it bonds *with the strange woman, does it not have the power to bond with a loving wife of covenant? If this is the case, can we consider sex to be a spiritual weapon?*

What then of the wife who is punished and ridiculed for not doing the things that the adulteress is more than willing to do? Should she subject herself to the abuse and emotional battering every time she has sex with her husband? (This has not been my experience, but I know women who have experienced such.) These are serious questions, but each person must work out the answers with God personally.

JOURNEYING DOWN DIVORCE LANE

Imagine, you're unhappily married and your husband is adamantly unfaithful and unwilling to commit to actions deemed necessary to restore trust, and build intimacy in the relationship. Note, I didn't say 'to make the marriage work.'

Furthermore, he refuses to come clean about his unfaithfulness -which did not begin with the act of sex…far less for dealing with the issues at hand toward any resolution- an action I deemed at the time as his attempt to 'have his cake and eat it too.'

There are many actions that led him to this place. In fact, many affairs start off as the emotional kind.

Although that was probably true, I understand now that this was a by-product of 'emotional foolishness' and 'self-loathing.' At the root of every issue is a heart matter. When we have chambers of our hearts that are closed to the love of God, there is much darkness in that part of our lives.

Sometimes, we build walls to protect ourselves from emotional pain and shame that keep people out, but they really box us in. As a result of deep, unhealed emotional wounds, there was an inability to deal with emotional issues in a mature way, or to see clearly. That pain and rejection colors and corrupts our vision.

These well-guarded, unhealed areas left an empty space where God's loving identity should have resided, resulting in a 'neediness' for affirmation from the 'other woman' because he felt so ill equipped to deal with marital issues.

The way we 'see' God affects our interaction with Him and His ability to reach our hearts. He won't force Himself upon us.

Apart from the infidelity, I felt at the time that there was nothing to hold on to or fight for given the way I was being treated.

I did not get to this point of seeking a divorce flippantly or without much struggle, as I genuinely desired to be married 'till death do us part.' It seemed like I was doing cartwheels, but nothing seemed to be enough. One person cannot carry a marriage.

For him, everything was my fault, and there was a refusal to seek counselling or professional help. He would say, "I am a private person, and I don't want people knowing my business." Somewhere along the way, he had decided that he was no longer a Christian without informing me, so he did not desire to go to a pastor for counselling, nor did he desire to pray with me.

I remember we had won a gift certificate at an event to attend a Family Life course geared towards married couples. We attended one evening and left early because "Those people had issues and all we needed to do is go out some more."

Let me say here that spiritual adultery takes place long before actual adultery does. If a man won't be faithful to God, he certainly won't be faithful to a wife. I've also noticed that adultery and emotional abuse go together. Wherever witchcraft is, there'll also be abuse of some form, accompanied by strife and confusion.

If your husband is being influenced by a spirit of witchcraft, he will exhibit certain behaviours that are almost textbook from person to person.

You will be treated with contempt as though you are the enemy. People on the outside would have nothing but great things to say about you though. He's lavish with his praise to everyone but you. Emotional abuse is very difficult to describe to people who have not experienced it themselves.

People often feel that one can stay in such a scenario because "D man not beatin' yuh and he providing. What yuh want again?" In some circles, there seems to be a mindset that one can 'just pray' and God will work it out. If nothing is done differently, nothing changes. In fact, things can actually get worse.

So many women, including pastors' wives suffer in silence because of this thinking. Then again, who do you go to? Just as with a festering sore, if it is not exposed, it cannot be healed.

Isn't is easier to deal with an issue than to bury it? My husband only admitted to his affair after we were already divorced. I never needed his confession to confirm what the spirit of God had already shown me.

I remember that there was a point where things were getting very scary for me. His attitude toward me got colder and colder. One day, he was speaking to a lady on the telephone about a customer query. I heard him become very abusive to her. I had never seen that type of aggression up until that point. That was when I made up my mind to leave.

This first time I left, we still lived abroad, and I had no intention of returning, but God… I tried seeking legal advice, to no avail. The doors never opened, despite my best efforts. God said to me that it was not over yet, and that I needed to return.

He had no clue until I got to Trinidad with our son that I never intended to return. It is amazing how many people are actually there to help you when you're in crisis. I thank God for those people He placed around me at the time. It was only when we got home that I had the conversation that I was not returning because I was fearful of what might have happened had I said it before my leaving. Whether this fear was justified or not is debatable. However, in my mind, it was very real, and I didn't risk saying anything until I'd arrived home safely.

He seemed genuinely startled at my disclosure, and promptly hopped on a plane home to 'keep his family together.' We had one session with our pastor before he left the country again to return to work.

I agreed to return to Barbados on three conditions:

1. Sever that inappropriate relationship
2. Transfer half ownership of the property bought to build our home to me
3. We both needed to do the work it took for our relationship to work. I was not willing to do it alone

Interestingly, 'his friend' had handled the paperwork for a matter of ours that needed attention. A situation had arisen where there was something that he needed to go back to her to get. I didn't make a fuss about it when he said that he would have to ask her for it. It was only obvious, and I expected that.

Sometime later, when we were moving ahead with plans to build, there was a matter that he had asked me about. For whatever reason, he thought that I wasn't moving fast enough on it, and he said to me that he asked 'his friend' to assist.

I said to him, "I thought we had an agreement," to which he replied, "That agreement was a stupid one to make. It was made under duress at the time. I felt that it was what I had to say. You can't deny me of all my friends or tell me who I can or cannot talk to. I felt so emasculated having to say to you that I had to go to her the last time." My response was, "It is very clear to me who your wife is and where your allegiance lies."

I had never been a jealous wife nor one who told him who he could or could not talk to. I had an issue with this person for good reason, and it was only after it came out that he had 'feelings' for this person, and we had the session with pastor, that I set condition 1.

The second condition was really the only one that remained, and the first to be met. Without going into too much detail, things worked for a while but quickly regressed.

I was amused post-divorce that he thought I'd hired a private investigator because of the questions I'd asked and the things I'd told him. God gave me dreams and showed me what I needed to know.

I think God wanted me to know when it did come to divorce that I had truly given my all towards having a healthy and harmonious relationship. He didn't want me to look back with any doubt in my mind as to whether I had done the right thing.

We returned to Trinidad in December 2006. Wouldn't you know, she had returned to Trinidad too? Eventually, they started seeing each other again. There is one incident that I recall when I was dropping him to the airport for a business trip, and he picked a fight ending in, "Screw you. I don't want to have anything to do with you." I know now it was out of guilt to justify what he was going to do on that trip.

As God would have it, He orchestrated for him to leave the house one evening with his email open. I had enough time to locate and print those travel plans and walk to my closet with it, before the door opened and he returned. He probably had remembered that he left it open, but never asked me anything.

Prior to this marital situation, I was not 'that woman' who invaded anyone's privacy by going through phones or emails, but I felt I had to do what I had to do at the time. He wasn't forthcoming with the truth, and had proven that he could not be trusted.

That incident on the way to the airport was my point of no return. I was no longer willing to try. I used to say to him, "If I'm crying and trying to talk, know that I care. When, I'm done, I'm done." I never wanted to get to that point. I drove to someone's place (who knew us both) after dropping him to the airport, and said to her, "He says he doesn't want to have anything to do with me, and now, I'm done."

On his return from that trip, he came home cool and normal, as though nothing had happened. He came into my bedroom, lay on the bed and asked me if everything was ok. I said, "No," and he asked what was wrong. I said, "I want a divorce."

I think this shocked him because he'd never expected me to go down this road. He asked me if I had thought it through...if I was sure. I responded in the affirmative. He asked me, "So you don't want to go to counselling?" "No, for what? I'm not willing anymore." At this stage, this sudden willingness to go to counselling, I felt was only about appearances because the illusion of a family was more desirable than another divorce. It really wasn't about wanting to be with me, or doing the work, and I was not willing to ride the roller coaster anymore. I think it was done so he could tell people that he asked me and I was unwilling, and I could be blamed for our divorce.

I knew who I was dealing with. In front of the counsellor, he would remain calm and say all the right things, and I would end up looking like a *basket case*! When we got home, nothing would change.

There was a day when it hit him that I was actually serious. He came home and said to me, "You came with nothing, leave with nothing. Pack your clothes and leave. Call your sister or someone to come for you, but don't be here when I get back or I'll put your things out." As scared as I was, I said calmly, "I'm not going anywhere." He took Chilo and left the house. I knew that he was trying to bully me into leaving so that he could say that I walked out and abandoned the marriage and our son. I didn't know that what he did was assault (until I made the police report, as I was advised to), but I just knew I was supposed to stand my ground.

Well, I got on the phone and called a relative and a friend who came with her husband, his friend. They were all there when he came back, and tried to talk some sense into him. I stayed there until it was the God appointed time for me to leave. He would actually be the one to propose that I move to the house in the valley to get our son settled in his new school.

To fast-forward, Mr. Ex never showed up for the divorce hearing. Although it hurt at the time, it was a blessing in disguise. Instead of opting to go to trial, we chose to settle in Family Court through mediation. It was certainly the more economic option, as there was no cost.

There were some questionable things that my lawyer was advising me to still bring up in the final hearing, but I just wanted it all to be over, and we had already sat and agreed on what was being presented.

I wanted my freedom and sanity, and I wanted our son to be as well-adjusted as he possibly could. As the magistrate said, "Sometimes, you have to give up some rights in favour of what you value more."

DIVORCE IS WORSE THAN DEATH

They say that "Divorce is worse than death…" I've actually been able to experience both first-hand and decide for myself.

The pain of my husband's death (yes, I said my husband and not my ex-husband- stay tuned for that explanation) was not to be compared to the pain of divorce.

Before, during and after divorce, I mourned my husband in many ways much more than I had mourned in his death. At the time of his death, I actually felt closest to him and was joyous in the midst of the sadness because he had surrendered his life to Jesus.

It was more torturous having to deal with him while dealing with the many phases of divorce pain and fall out on a personal level… the rejection, the anger, the self-blame and questioning, the other women, the judgements of others, the shame, feelings of worthlessness and being undesirable, protecting our son and financial and logistical adjustments.

With divorce, we still needed to communicate because we had a son. It was not always pleasant or easy… but with God, it got better, however until that happened, it was very painful to have to interact, especially when it felt like you were being treated with contempt.

I will say though the process between divorce and death certainly transformed me in ways that may not have happened otherwise.

It killed me, it brought me back to life and God used it to show me my worth and who I truly was and *who I truly* am created to be.

I learnt that he wouldn't change until I first allowed God to change me.

Humility moves more mountains than self-preservation ever could. Letting go is often more powerful than holding on.

I learnt to see him as a human being who God loved- just as much as me, I might add. This changed my prayers. God held a mirror up and showed me that there is no big sin and little sin in His eyes and that I fell short every day, yet He's been merciful.

WHY GOD HATES DIVORCE

We always hear that God hates divorce, but very rarely do we hear why...very rarely do we hear His heart on the matter. Even though He does give instances where divorce is permissible (adultery/desertion/abuse), His preference is reconciliation. He understands the pain that comes from adultery having experienced it over and over with His people. Yet, the story of Hosea gives us a picture of the type of love He has for us.

Why?

Firstly, God is Love...not the kind of love that we have which is self-*ish* at best, but the unconditional kind. His love is the kind that will sacrifice and die for us. He never leaves us or forsakes us, no matter what we do or how far we go away from Him. He forgives us when we repent and receives us again unto Himself.

The very essence of God is reconciliation, so much so that He sacrificed His Son, Himself in order to reconcile us to Himself. So, to ask Him to sanction divorce is to ask Him to go against the very essence of who He is; it's asking Him to rip His heart out, to not be Himself. If He's to compromise Himself in this way, shouldn't it stand to reason that He could compromise in other areas as well? He could then, not hold to His other promises as well, couldn't He? Then, He wouldn't be God because we couldn't trust Him to be true to His word. Marriage is the relationship God likens His relationship with the church to.

So, to divorce He says, it wasn't His intention but because of the hardness of our hearts (inability to truly forgive), go ahead in these instances; however, either be reconciled to your husband or remain unmarried till death. (I Corinthians 7: 10-11, 39) Tough word, right? Is it tough to receive all the promises He made to us? Don't we all need His grace because we fail Him daily?

I remember when I was going through my divorce, God would say to me, "Pray for him," and I would reply, "What will I pray for him that I haven't already prayed." Later on, I realised that God is the initiator of prayer, and if He asks us to pray, He is willing to lead and He also desires to do something in our lives.

One thing that happened when I began to pray is a softening of my heart. I grew in compassion, but God also changed my prayer. I also began to pray for him as a hurt, lost person who God loved and not a wicked spouse. I was no longer praying a selfish prayer for him to change because I wanted to be happy. I prayed for an individual and not a marriage. For, marriage is not an entity unto itself, but a covenant between two whole individuals.

One day, as I was having a rant with the Lord, He took me to the story of Jonah. He asked me a couple questions, "Why are you upset because I choose to show mercy on him, when I've shown you so much? Do you think that I love you more than him or that you deserve my mercy more? I will show mercy on whom I will." The Lord showed me that He is merciful to me every day, and that my sins aren't any smaller than his. In God's eyes, sin is sin because His standards and thoughts are so much higher than ours.

When I understood that I was no better than him and that God loved him just as much as me, I was able to have compassion. God had me eat some serious humble pie there.

I understood just how much God loved each of us and the lengths He would go to reconcile with us.

When God covenants with us, it's forever. He doesn't think about what if it doesn't work out. He doesn't divorce us or walk out on us when we aren't who He expects us to be. He doesn't withhold His love when we don't measure up.

The word says that obedience is better than sacrifice, but I've learnt that sometimes, **obedience is the sacrifice,** and that sacrifice is what will cause others to see Him. The world is watching and waiting for someone to walk out this love of God that they're always hearing about.

This sacrifice also causes us to see Him as He truly is. There are some things we never get a revelation of or come to know unless we surrender our will to His and make the sacrifice.

OBEDIENCE IS THE SACRIFICE

There has been much revelation in recent years about love languages and having sensitivity and appreciation for the way our significant others perceive, receive and feel loved.

Do we know how God perceives, receives and feels loved? Have we given it much thought?

Well, we can be certain of it because He actually tells us. He tells us that if we love Him, we will obey His commands. Put another way, I feel loved and know you love me when you do what I ask you to. God's love language is obedience.

How many of us know that it is way easier said than done? The things God asks us to do can be very difficult. They can often go against our natural inclination or thinking, and we don't always feel to. We weren't called to live by feelings though, but by faith, or else it would be impossible to please Him. It would also be impossible to do what He requires in and of us.

It may seem a harsh thing when God says that obedience is better than sacrifice.

"So, Lord, you mean that you would rather I obey in one thing than I do many things to show you that I love you?"

"YES!!!"

The good news is that He is quite prepared and willing to help us do what He's asking us to do. In fact, He knows that we need Him and with Him, nothing shall be impossible. Our Father actually wants us to win, He's destined us to. Consequently, when we ask Him to help us do that thing He requires of us, He probably wants to more than we want Him to.

This is why He says, when we ask anything according to His will, He will do it. He rushes to perform His will.

Our way can seem so much easier, and we can try to avoid doing that 'hard thing' by substituting a bunch of easier ones, but God knows… We can't run or hide from Him, especially when it comes to matters of the heart.

I remember my deceased husband and I having a conversation once about all these things that he was 'killing himself' doing for me and the family and how unappreciative I seemed to be. My response was that I had never asked him to do those things. You see, I wanted his heart and I probably had a different love language.

So, I didn't perceive, receive or feel loved by the things he was sacrificially doing for me. It's not that they didn't matter because they were important, but not when it came to matters of my heart.

We may argue that we've done all these things in His name, for Him, and in the end, they won't matter because they weren't the things He asked for. Furthermore, He may perceive that they weren't even done in love because He has a different love language: ***OBEDIENCE.***

So, if we've done it all and had no love, it would have been for naught and our sacrifices would have been unacceptable. In His words, He would say, "Depart from me, I never knew you." (Ref. Matthew 7:21-23) Obedience is the thing that says to God, "I Love You." OBEDIENCE IS THE SACRIFICE He requires, but it is a heart matter. The only acceptable sacrifice is one done in love, (the kind that does not seek itself) and that means obedience.

Lastly, our Heavenly Father is not a task master just sitting up in heaven and giving us a bunch of Do's and Don'ts. Our desire to obey should be out of a heart of genuine love for Him. He paid a sacrifice for us with His life, and He did it out of love. He asks, "Your life for mine."

When we know His love, it's really hard not to want to please Him. (He loved you before you even had a thought about Him and it wasn't dependent on anything you did or didn't do.) If this is not your motivation or experience, ask the Father to give you an encounter with His love. He wants nothing more than to be known by you. This is a desire of His heart and He longs to grant it if it becomes a desire of yours.

Reflections:

1. Is there something that you know in your heart God has been asking you to do? List

2. Why have you hesitated in following through?
3. Why do you think God has asked this of you?
4. Do you think He means you harm?
5. What do you think He thinks about you?
6. What are all your thoughts about God?
7. What is the source of these thoughts?
8. Do you doubt God's ability or faithfulness to see you through?

9. Could your beliefs about God be hindering you from being obedient and having a deeper relationship with Him?

10. Could your thoughts about yourself be hindering you from obeying God?

11. Is the Bible the Word of God, or just a book about Him?

12. Are the words of the Bible True or Truth?

Exercise:

1. For every thought about yourself, match it against what you believe God says? Do they agree?

2. What does the Word actually say about you?

3. How do you feel and what do you believe about what the Word says?

4. For every belief about God, match it against what the Word of God says? Do they agree?

DIVORCE DISCOURSE

When I got married, divorce was never an option in my mind. Who knew that years later, I would find myself as a divorcee and single-mother? The decision to divorce, however is something I believe God permitted me to do.

There has been ongoing debate in Christendom as to whether divorce is permitted, the grounds on which it is and whether divorced persons may remarry.

I can only share from my experience with God, what He said to me in context of what His word says and my understanding of it. Each person must walk it out with God. I have seen remarried couples who are being used mightily by God. It is not for me to say that God did not sanction their relationship.

When I reflect, I've wondered whether I should have just separated given the way things later unfolded. Stay with me though, we'll get to that…

GROUNDS:

And I say unto you, whoever divorces his wife, except for sexual immorality, and marries another, commits adultery; and whoever marries her who is divorced, commits adultery. Matthew 19:9

…Whoever divorces his wife, let him give her a certificate of divorce. But I say to you that whoever divorces his wife for any reason except sexual immorality causes her to commit adultery;

and whoever marries a woman who is divorced commits adultery. Matthew 5:31-32

But to the rest I, not the Lord, say: If any brother has a wife who does not believe, and she is willing to live with him, let him not divorce her. And a woman who has a husband who does not believe, if he is willing to live with her, let her not divorce him. For the unbelieving husband is sanctified by the wife, and the unbelieving wife is sanctified by the husband...but if the unbeliever departs, let him depart; a brother or a sister is not under bondage in such cases. But God has called us to peace. I Corinthians 7:12-15

In my understanding at that time, both infidelity and abuse were grounds for divorce. Abuse constituted "Not dwelling together in peace," and even though, we were physically living together, in effect, he had already left our marriage. (There was no forsaking all others for me, no remorse, no honest communication and no real effort at making things work. One person does not *'a marriage make'*.) In addition, he was an unbeliever who had left, so I was not bound. Important to note here: it matters not what someone calls himself, we know a tree by its fruit.

I remember feeling as though I couldn't wait for my divorce to be final, so that I could see other people. Up until the time that I'm writing this chapter, it's been nine years and I'm still waiting...

After my divorce became final in 2010, the Lord said to me, *"You either reconcile with him, or stay by yourself until death parts you."* I said to God, "You've got to be kidding me. After I go through all that I did, and you permitted me to leave him, how could you ask this of me? You mean, he gets to do what he wants and see who he wants still, and I have to stay by myself? That's not fair!"

"Now to the married, I command, yet not I but the Lord: A wife is not to depart from her husband. But even if she does depart, let her remain unmarried or be reconciled to her husband. And a husband is not to divorce his wife… A wife is bound by law as long as her husband lives; but if her husband dies, she is at liberty to be married to whom she wishes, only in the Lord." I Corinthians 7:10-11, 39

These verses haunted me. They were everywhere I turned, it seemed. I couldn't escape. I cried and pleaded with the Lord to release me, and I looked for every sermon and every scripture to let me off this hook, but found none. I could not continue to fight with God for too long, for it is not a battle I would ever win.

This was the most difficult word I'd ever had to receive from the Lord (up until that time), but from the moment I surrendered, it began to transform my life in a way like no other has to date. It is the thing that has brought me into a deeper understanding of the love God has for us and the sacrifice He made.

His sacrifice could not have been made on 'feelings,' but He chose to love. Our feelings can follow our will, and we can love anyone we want to. It's all in the letting go.

I asked God to help me to want what He wanted, so that when that reconciliation time came, I would not have been doing it under duress. I wanted to be happy in doing His will, and I wanted to be happy in my marriage relationship.

He said to me that my husband would be a new creature in Christ (II Corinthians 5:17-18) and that He wasn't asking me to trust him, but to trust Him.

**Heart Matter #1: Trusting Him with my whole heart.
By this, I settled in my heart that if God was going to save him and transform him, then we'd be ok because we would both be submitted to His will, and He would keep us.

ARE THERE GROUNDS FOR RE-MARRIAGE?

I've found grounds for divorce, but even with those, God says that His desire is reconciliation.

These are the scriptures on re-marriage:
Luke 16:18; Matthew 19:8-9; Mark 10:11-12

The only grounds for re-marriage I've found are predicated on the first spouse being dead, as in I Corinthians 7:39. That being said, I believe every person has to work it out with God in his/her specific situation.

SCRIBAL PURGING

As in my teenage years, writing would serve to be very cathartic during the trauma of emotional abuse, adultery, separation, divorce and post-divorce singlehood.

What follows are verses and songs written over the years, as I was 'going through?' They reflect my thoughts and emotions at the time when they were written. In some cases, they were written post conversation or event.

BACKSTAGE STORY

People see you everyday
They think you are so charming
Just because you smile a lot
And call everyone darling.
But they don't live with you
They just do have a clue
What goes on 'off-stage'
The evil things you say and do.

CHORUS:
You don't hit me, I'm so glad...
But words and coldness hit me just as hard
I know I'm not losing my mind
For too long I have been so blind
Love does not equal control
Off this coaster, I must roll.

Vs.
And let's not talk about your 'friends'
The women you keep close
Who think that they should have you-
Their lives could be much worse
Maybe, I would be better off
But, I'm just cursed you see
Because I really love you
What the hell is wrong with me?

BRIDGE:
This life with Jekyll and Hyde
Keeps weighing on me
Sucking all my life
I'm acting like a zombie
Reflecting on a time
Of what I used to be
Someone, please won't you help me?

(Chorus)

Vs.
Walking on eggshells-takes more strength to stay
It would be easier to pack and run away
Yet you call me weak and passive
The pain that my heart feels is massive.
Yet, I promised God, I'd try
But will you break me till I die?

SELF-TALK

Why are you still trying to make it work
With someone who has already left?
His body is still near
But his heart is far away.
And if he wants to go
There is nothing you can do
To make him stay.

You try to break through
But the wall is still there-
No matter what you do.
You say, "If only he could see...?"
Still trying to make me think
Something's wrong with me.

I did not see or have the proof
But I felt her presence, I knew it...
At times when we were intimate.
Can't explain it, couldn't fight it
Prayed to God to illuminate.

God wanted me to choose
To forsake all for Him.
To show me who I am,
So, healing could begin.
The revelation, in time it came.

Chorus:
Thank you Lord, you're so good to me
You keep loving me no matter what.
You taught me who I am
Took me 'Out the Box'
And all I can say is thank you.

THE FINAL LETTER

Dr. Jekyll, Mr. Hyde,
Who am I dealing with today?
You say you love me
Yet, how can you treat me this way?
You chose to leave and yet
You want me to stay.
How long can this go on?

Still trying to make things work
When you're already gone
Fighting a losing battle
Cause she's already won.
Been trying God's way...
Forgive, Pray, Believe, Stay
But you don't live with me in peace
So, it's time to go our separate ways.

Tormented, fragmented...
Wanna make me into you.
Accusing me of all you are
Blinded by untruth.
No more questions now,
Decisions I have made.
To lose myself, I now know how
I'm done with this charade.

God is my only source
For everything I need.
Jesus, my all, He came to die
To set the captives free.
There's nothing you can do
That He can't do for me
More abundantly, I might add

His MO's to exceed.
So, peace to you
I'm done with this.
I question what I'm going to miss.
Not the criticism, mind games and the lies
Nor the many nights
I lay in bed and cried.
The God I serve
Would never give me less than I deserve.

To save myself I must
For our love was sacrificed
On an altar of lust.
What an utter betrayal of my trust.

THE AFFAIR

You think that you're happy
But you're not
You'll never be satisfied
With what you've got
And when you realise
What you think she is, she's not
It'll be too late.

What makes you think you're special?
You don't even have a clue
The very same thing he did to me,
He'll do to you
The only difference is,
No respect will be due.

So maybe, you deserve each other
Drowning in a sea of lust
Trying to build on broken trust
Lies, deceit and oh so lost
Ever learning, truth unknown
Unaware of what you truly yearn.

Don't you know you're not in control?
Life is not yours to hold
And karma is a bitch
The hole you tried to dig for me
For you, will be a big ditch
Be careful what you sow...

Reality bites like a pit bull
So, I hope you've got your gloves
Cause true love cannot be feigned
Without none, respect cannot be gained
Put your trust in someone higher
Become someone I can admire.

Chorus:

The answer lies within
Can't be happy off
Someone else's tears
Stop justifying wrong
Only hurt comes from affairs

THE BETRAYAL

Under a spell
His darkness covered me.
My light grew dim
Overshadowed by
The pain he felt within.

I lost my hope, my joy
Devoured on the altar of his pride
But, the still small voice broke through inside
I heard myself scream out
Enough! I must return to my love.

My God, I strayed so far from you
Only your love ever proved true.
Left you to pursue an illusion
My life ever changed by that decision.
Who am I when I'm not with you?

Left you for a man... You, he didn't know
Thinking, you would make it so.
But as his wife,
The wrong things grew 1000 times.
Done in by his grand disguise.

Your words, he despised
And tried to pick them apart...
Questioning and challenging
It cut straight through my heart.
All we had consumed on his lust
Now offended by the name of Jesus.

How wrong was I, My Lord?
My friend, my first love…
I give you my desires, my heart
So sorry for the time we spent apart.
Can we try again?
I want my light to shine
For what's yours is truly mine.

CAN'T GET RIGHT BY DOING WRONG

Intro
I never thought that I would be
An unfaithful husband...

Vs.
When we met, it was so easy to talk to yuh-
We had a connection...I questioned whether
My love for my wife was true
It was unfair to find solace
In your bedroom... with you.

Bridge:
I took advantage of your weakness
Oh, sin can be such bliss
I should have stopped at the very first kiss

Chorus:
Now I know,
Shudda known better
Shudda been strong
Can't get right by doing wrong

Vs.
I realise now anything worthwhile
Requires work and dedication
Temptation comes quickly to beguile
And with challenges come introspection.
Thanks for holding a mirror to my eyes
So, I could see through all the lies.

(Chorus)

Vs.
I was expecting perfection in my wife
Denying imperfections in my life
Now I see the need for change,
So, I look to God above
To become a man
Who deserves her love.

STRUNG ALONG

Don't know what I was expecting
I just really loved your company.
I fooled myself into thinking
"We're good friends-
That's all I want to be."

Chorus:
The fog has cleared
And now I can see
Stopped blaming you and looked at me
Now love myself enough to know
God used us to make me grow

Like a dog trying to catch its tail
The secret calls, emotional e-mails
I stayed- hoping for a miracle-
Knowing you were unavailable
I failed to see the obvious...
You did nothing to discourage us.

(Chorus)

How was I supposed to know
Tux was bought - marriage was a go?
You really dogged me out you know
The boundaries you did not draw.

Can't help but feel betrayed and used
Mixed signals kept me torn and confused
Please know that you I will not hate
I've learnt to accept my fate.

Bridge:
If I knew then what I do now
What went down between us
I'd never allow

WHERE IS YOUR GOD?

Gave up my life to follow you...
Now nothing I do makes sense
My feelings don't seem to matter now
You'll work everything out, somehow.

Where is your God, they say,
I thought He was the one
Who brought you all this way
If all you seem to do is pray,
How come nothing's going your way?

If He's so mighty, strong and true
How come He's not taking care of you?
You must be doing something wrong
For Him to suffer you for so long.

But I, Lord I believe your word
You will never forsake me.
You took me through the wilderness
To prove that I belong to you

I will not have to fight, You said
For the battle is yours instead.
Stand, my child, just stand
And watch me make my entrance grand.

All the tongues, I'll silence them
For my blessings will overtake you
Like a flood, my spirit will engulf you
And they shall be afraid
But they will see your God is true.

I AM THE LORD

You are one, but not alone
Through your obedience
Many will know
Who I am, who I am
I am the Lord.

CHORUS:

I am the Lord, I am the Lord
Know I am the Lord
I AM...

So, give it up, don't think it hard
From your sacrifice,
Blessings will flow
Not long again,
Not far to go
I am the Lord.

You've come too far
You cannot quit
I know you're weak
But I will do it
When you're weak
I am strong
I am the Lord; I am the Lord.

I know you wonder, if I hear
You start to doubt
When you don't feel me near
I promised you
I'll never leave

I am the Lord.

There is nothing you need to fear
Who can hurt you,
When I am there?
I love you child
You are mine
I am your Lord.

FROM JONAH'S HEART TO MINE

The Lord had me reading about Jonah one day to show me my 'heart condition.' Jonah is sent as a prophet of the Lord to 'cry against' the city of Nineveh. The king decreed a fast and the people obeyed and repented of their evil ways.

As a result, we are told that God decided to spare them from His judgement. Jonah became very angry, and wished for death. He departed from the city and threw himself a pity party under a booth which he made for himself.

The Lord in His mercy caused a gourd to grow up to overshadow Jonah and deliver him from his grief. This made him happy indeed, until the next morning when God caused a worm to bring about the withering of the gourd. In addition, God caused the sun to beat down on Jonah's head and the wind to blow violently.

Jonah again wishes for death. Then, the Lord asks him, "Do you have a right to be angry for the gourd?" to which Jonah answers in the affirmative.

Then, the Lord says to him, "You've had pity on the gourd for which you did nothing to cause it to grow, and which grew up in a night and died in a night. Should I not spare Nineveh where more than 120,000 people who don't know their right hand from their left live?"

There was a period of time when I was going through the pain of the adultery and separation and I actually wished for the death of my husband. Imagine that… I'm not proud of it, but I want to be real with you about where my heart was at the time.

I felt as though he was causing so much pain in the lives of those who were supposed to matter that he just shouldn't be alive. It seemed as though he was walking around just doing what he wanted and the Lord was not dealing with him. I wanted vengeance, justice, vindication. He should pay for what he'd done.

So, the Lord asked me these questions when I had read Jonah's story:

1. Why are you angry because I choose to have mercy on him when I've been so merciful to you?

2. Do you think that I love you more than I love him?

3. Do you think that you've done something to earn or deserve my mercy?

I have been accused by my husband of being self-righteous before. Never in my mind would I have believed that there was any truth to that statement... until the Lord asked me those questions.

He held a mirror up to me and showed me that I fell short every single day, yet I was still walking around with His breath in my nostrils. He showed me that in His eyes, there is no big sin or little sin. Therefore, as wicked as I would have liked to label my husband, in God's eyes, I would have been labelled the same were it not for the blood of Jesus.

There was nothing that I did better to deserve the love and grace of my Lord. I was just as ignorant, just as lost and just as broken. Someone prayed for me, someone believed in me, and someone had mercy on me. What if the Lord had not been patient with me?

There are those that we love to hate because we think that we are 'not like them,' but from where our Father sits, all the 'good' we do is nothing without a 'heart transplant.' Ephesians 3:17-19; 2:8-10

MERCIFUL NOT VENGEFUL

I will have mercy on whom I will, and I will have compassion on whom I will (Romans 9:15)

Vengeance is mine, I will repay (Romans 12:19)

This whole journey has made one aspect of God's nature very clear. He really does not want any of us to perish. He is very merciful and patient with us. He gives us every possible opportunity to come to Him and relentlessly pursues our hearts.

The other thing is that the prayers of His children never go in vain. This translates to His word never returns void because His children are those who carry His heart. So, their prayers start with Him, and He watches over His word to ensure it happens.

When my husband got his CBC results, the doctor indicated that he was surprised that he was still walking around because healthier people were dropping down. I saw the hand of God from the time of his diagnosis to the point where he breathed his last breath. He was shown favour by his company, by doctors and hospitals at home and abroad.

If God hadn't been merciful to me, I wouldn't be here to tell this story.

FORGIVENESS- IS IT TRULY POSSIBLE?

Firstly, let's look at what forgiveness means on a basic level.

The Wikipedia Definition: "**Forgiveness *is*** the **intentional** and **voluntary** process by which a victim undergoes a change in feelings and attitude regarding an offense, **let's go** of negative emotions such as vengefulness, with an increased ability to wish the offender well."

The simple answer to whether forgiveness is truly possible is Absolutely, YES!!! It is truly possible, for with God, nothing is impossible.

The process, however is a bit more complex. The one thing worth noting is that Forgiveness is intentional and voluntary. It is a matter of the *Will*, and it boils down to will you or won't you, regardless of initial feelings. It requires decisive action.

That decisive action must have its foundation in Truth and Love...Jesus. More than His word (which He embodies) is the relationship that we have with Him. When we love Him, we have a sincere desire to please Him- if we love, we obey. His love, never fails, but we must trust Him with our ENTIRE heart, knowing that we (our hearts) are safe with Him always. Our wills are to be surrendered to Him only, otherwise, we may build up resentment as 'The arm of flesh will always fail.'

Resentment will not take root when our being and doing originate from a heart of God's love.

Power belongs to whomever we surrender our wills. If we don't *will* to do what He wills (which is surrender to Him), then we surrender to another. Unforgiveness is like a ball and chain. If we fail to release others, then we remain bound and controlled by them. This can be a form of idolatry because we make this offense or this person elevated above God and His goodness.

Whatever is not of faith is of fear. Faith comes by 'hearing' the WORD of God. So, if we aren't operating in faith in the Word/God, we are operating in self which would be prideful and fear-based operation where we try to 'protect' ourselves from being controlled and manipulated or to avoid pain and suffering.

There's no way to be a true disciple of Christ and escape pain and suffering, but we know that when we die with Him, we live in and through Him. Control and manipulation are about fear and by extension pride, so they can't be combated with fear-based actions, but actually in humility- letting go to Christ and resting or trusting in Him alone. Then, He is able to fight for us.

The things we fear come upon us. So, the more we try to avoid what we don't want because of fear, it attracts it to ourselves. Fear has torment. How we get rid of it is displacement with the living word. *Perfect love casts out all fear. I John 4:18*

Sometimes, it can seem like we are allowing the perpetrator to 'get away with,' prosper or walk all over us, but when we know to whom we are submitting, we draw strength to endure, and we know that we are triumphant. We may even in the midst of the pain (because it is certainly not always an easy thing), find pleasure in knowing that we are pleasing the true lover of our souls, and His peace will prevail. This is particularly true in marriage- the relationship God most likens our relationship with Him to.

What forgiveness develops in us are compassion and the God kind of love, the unconditional kind- which the world needs to see.

"Father, forgive them, for they know not what they do."
Luke 23:34

Remember David and Saul? Despite all that Saul did to David (even attempted murder), David did not retaliate, but chose to still honour Saul unto God- knowing that God had chosen Saul (rebellious or not, anointing or no more anointing). Sometimes, God will send us someone or something to attack our identity to get self out of us.

We should not have a self to defend because we should already be dead in Christ.

Every time offenses come, they are opportunities to die some more, grow in God's love some more and ultimately to have more of His power manifested in and through us.

Resurrection power cannot be made manifest in a vessel that is alive.

His strength is made perfect in our weakness. (2 Corinthians 12:9) It's not about what is fair or being right, but about His righteousness and our obedience to Him. Once we stand on the Rock, the Rock will hold us up.

Besides, in Daddy's kingdom, forgiveness is not an option. Even though it is intentional and not dependent on the other person, we can't be OK without embracing it. We can't say we love God and not be forgiving.

"For if you forgive men their trespasses, your heavenly Father will also forgive you. But if you do not forgive men their trespasses, neither will your Father forgive yours."
Matthew 6:14-15

Forgiveness doesn't always happen once and for all, often it happens in stages, and we do the 'seventy times seven,' but with Him, all things are possible. Our Father doesn't expect us to try to forgive on our own. In fact, He knows we need His help...we need God Power. Let us 'harden not our hearts' and trust in the ONE, who is greater than anything we could ever face.

Finally, brethren, whatever things are true, whatever things are noble, whatever things are just, whatever things are pure, whatever things are lovely, whatever things are of good report, if there is any virtue and if there is anything praiseworthy – meditate on these things. The things which you learned and received and heard and saw in me, these do, and the God of peace will be with you.
Philippians 4:8-9.

RECONCILIATION

The Oxford dictionary meaning of reconciliation is as follows:

1. An end to a disagreement and the start of good relationship again

2. The process of making it possible for two different ideas, facts, etc. to exist together without being opposed to each other.

Did my ex-husband and I reconcile? The answer is emphatically, "Yes." Post-divorce, we probably became better friends than we ever were, and we shared a mutual respect for each other. There could be no reconciliation without forgiveness, but how do we know when we've truly forgiven?

I've often heard the expression "Forgive and forget," but do we ever forget though? Realistically speaking, I may still remember an incident, but that doesn't mean that I haven't forgiven. I think we know when we've forgiven when we no longer feel any pain or experience any anger or offense when we do remember.

CHANGE FOR A CHANGE

The love of God has the power to transform the hardest of hearts. When we are open to Him, He is able to heal our brokenness and make us into a brand-new vessel.

As we become love-filled, we become potent tools in His hands to bring transformation to the lives of others. This is the power of a surrendered heart.

God's love never fails. When we have received unconditional love, we become more compassionate and are able to be patient with the struggles of others.

Submission is a curse word to some because they don't understand how it works in the kingdom. It does not mean that we become doormats. Rather, it means that we choose to turn the matter over to a capable God by honouring His word. Submission to God is a power play. It is in our time of weakness that God can show Himself strong. There is strength in humility and vulnerability.

Our focus should be in honouring God and not what the other person is doing or how we feel. God's opinion is the only one that matters. Our joy and peace come from doing His will. This may mean acquiescing to your husband in a contrary (not sinful) decision, or it may mean praying for and blessing someone who you know has ill intentions toward you.

Letting go allows God to take the wheel. He can't work to change the situation until we release our hold, self-effort and striving.

True transformation is an act of God, not done through our might or power. When we get into trying to change others, we move into manipulation and witchcraft.

As we focus on becoming who Father created us to be, then we will begin to see the change in others we desire. Better yet, we will begin to see true transformation into the image of Christ.

Just as couples who are intimately connected begin to resemble each other, so too we who are intimately connected to Christ begin to reflect His nature. People who spend great amounts of time together, rub off on each other.

Listen more and talk less. People tell us their issues. Post death, I saw that my deceased husband was way ahead of me in his seeing the Religious System for what it is. He wasn't fighting against God, but against the religious system. I remember being told that I was self-righteous and judgmental. Years later, those words would prove to be true.

I had placed myself above him, as though I was somehow better than he was because of my supposed position in Christ. There is nothing I did to deserve salvation. Every day, I fall short, and God has and continues to be merciful to me.

CHANGES

When my heart changes, my thoughts change…
When my thoughts change, my behaviour changes,
My words change, my world changes…
Everything around me changes.
Change begins with me?
Change My Heart Lord.

Often, the change we want to see is dependent on the change we need to be.

CHANGE ME LORD

Change Me Lord, Change Me
I'm the one that's in the way of me
Change me Lord, Change me
Till I reflect you only
So busy fixing someone else
That I forgot to check myself
Thank You for your mercy Lord, Change me

Sorry Lord, Sorry
Who am I that I should glory?
Search me Lord, Search me
Take pride and lust away
Open my eyes to see my filth
Humble me to seek your face
Sorry, please forgive me Lord, Sorry

Help me Lord, Help me
Break free from chains that hinder me
Help me Lord, Help me
To please you and you only
Help me stop pleasing someone else
To seek you wholly for myself
Help my mind to know that I am free, Help me.

Strengthen me Lord, Strengthen
To believe all you have said of me
Strengthen me Lord
My mind gets in the way
If you believe I can, I will
There's no one who can stop your plan
Your strength makes me unstoppable, My Lord

Hide me lord, Hide me
In your presence, I have all I need
Hide me, Lord, Hide me
From fakes and enemies
Please clothe me in my nakedness
Defend me with your mighty fist
Hide me in the valley Lord, Hide Me.

Break Down:
Blinded by my pride, I couldn't see
Three other fingers pointing back at me.
Pointing fingers, asking questions
Crying out for your direction
Then softly, your mercy fell afresh on me.

Outro:
Change me Lord, Change me
Till all I am is all you are
Till all I am is all you are
Change me.

There are many changes I saw in my deceased husband post-divorce, and I was able to see so much in him that I admire. In my place of pain, I was unable to appreciate or even see his many admirable qualities. Most of the transformation happened first in my heart though with God's help.

UNEARTHED DIAMONDS

Here are some things I've learnt post-divorce and having submitted myself to the *'bound till death'* Word. Like diamonds, these nuggets came from much pressure and tough times:

1.) WE CAN'T CHANGE OTHERS

We can only change ourselves- and even in that, we so need God's help.
I used to bend backwards trying to change and do things differently to please my husband. No matter what I did, it was never enough. I also said and did things to manipulate him into being who I wanted him to be.

Manipulation sounds very sinister, but we can do it without even being aware that we are manipulating. It can be very subtle, but at the end of the day, it's about us having our own way.

No matter how much I tried to change for my husband, it was never enough because he wasn't sure about who he was either. I wound up not knowing who I was and feeling like I was not enough.

It's important to KNOW WHO WE ARE before joining to another.

WE SHOULD BE COMPLETE AND HAPPY IN OUR SINGLENESS.

KNOWING OUR IDENTITY IS PARAMOUNT. Our change should be governed by God and a desire to be all He created us to be, and not people pleasing. This is why I don't believe in just pre-marital counseling. I think we should go through wholeness counseling before even considering a lifelong relationship, and I've submitted myself to this.

2.) DON'T COMPROMISE VALUES OR BELIEFS

Compromises made pre-marriage often come back to haunt us in marriage. Most issues pre-marriage are magnified in marriage and not the other way around. Be careful what you permit or turn a blind eye to. If we don't value our faith, no one else will. If we compromise so easily on something that is supposed to be important to us, it sends a message.

For me, I had pre-marital sex, thinking that we were going to get married anyway. Big mistake…I won't go into this one in great depth, but I will say that everything God says or has in place is for our own protection.

Holding out would have allowed me to see so many things much clearer, and I would have gotten to know the person better. Abstinence saves us from much heartache. Side note: The sex I've had in marriage was the best I've ever had because I felt safe and uninhibited. This person was mine, right?

The word of God says that sexual sin, unlike all the others affects us within and not without. Sex is not just a physical act, but it's a bonding agent. The two become one in body, mind, will and emotions. A soul tie is formed. That's why it's so difficult to break off some relationships even though we know we should.

3) MARRIAGE DOESN'T MAKE SOMEONE FAITHFUL

We need to be SINGLE and faithful first. By single, I mean being complete and happy without anyone. This goes for both men and women. We must know that we are loved and valuable on our own and be faithful to God… not needing anyone to validate who we are.

4) WE CAN'T MAKE A PERSON STAY WITH US IF THAT PERSON DOESN'T WANT TO

Try as we might, someone has to want a relationship with us and be willing to work at it, forsaking all others in order for it to work.

5) GOD DOESN'T LOVE US OR THE 'INJURED' PARTY MORE THAN THE PERSON WHO INFLICTED THE WOUND

Often the person inflicting the wound has personal hurt, turmoil and issues. God's grace is extended to that person as well because we all have fallen short. There's no big sin or little sin. Often, God uses us to extend that grace and to mirror His love if we allow Him to heal our hurt and help us to forgive. Greater love has no one than a person's life lain down for a friend.

6) FORGIVENESS OFTEN HAPPENS IN STAGES

We ought not to be too hard on ourselves. Sometimes, *we* think we have forgiven, and then something happens to make us realise that we're not quite there yet. Be patient with yourself and keep surrendering it to God.

Forgiveness and letting go are for us, but they also allow the other person to know and experience God's grace and His unconditional love. I've been told, "I don't even know why you still speak to me." We have the power through our surrender to God to cause people's hearts to begin to open up to His love and to begin to 'hear' or receive His word.

7) DON'T GET EVEN, GET HEALED

There is a point where we desire vindication, but God can change our heart if we're willing, and we can get to the point of compassion. It is possible to get to a point where we no longer feel sad or angry, but we have compassion for a person who is lost or broken and who needs to have a love encounter with God. We begin to see people as human beings or even friends separate from the pain of the past or even the present.

8) THERE IS ONE SOURCE

God is our only SOURCE- not our jobs, not our husbands, not other people, not money we can see, not the bank, Only God. When we really grasp this, it will empower us beyond measure. It is a very freeing thing to know that you don't need to be obligated to anyone or anything, but that you can be free to operate in obedience to what God said, knowing that He'll take care of you. He knows what we need and promises to supply all when we put Him first- His will, His righteousness. He also provides for whatever He wants us to do in His timing.

9) ROOT PRODUCES FRUIT

It is important to understand what drew you to the person you married and them to you. What is it in me? Unless, you work this out with God, you will continue to attract similar types with the same root issue. They may seem different at first, but will be same at the root.

10) HEALTHY BOUNDARIES ARE IMPORTANT

The more we allow God to love us and make us whole, these become obvious. It won't come naturally at first, but God…

11) PAIN OFTEN BIRTHS PURPOSE

God uses these traumatic life events to bring us to a deeper place in Him and often to birth PURPOSE. We learn most about who we are, what makes us happy and fulfilled. He can use every situation for our good and the good of those we love as well

12) WE WON'T MOVE ON WITHOUT MAKING PEACE

We won't get that breakthrough or get to move on until we learn the lesson and make peace. We can't have God's best outside of His will, so quit fighting Him and work with Him. Beauty is pain. Often used differently, but it works here too. No pain, no gain, it's only for a time

13) GOD IS FAITHFUL

God is who He says He is and will do what He says He will do. How can I say this? I've put Him and His word to the test. He says He can't be separated from His word and He watches over it to perform it.

Faith only grows when we exercise it. The proof is in taking the risk to believe and behave as though the bible is His word (in other words, having faith). He does nothing except by faith, so the only way to know is to try Him by faith.

I've been in so many 'hopeless' situations where there was nothing I or anyone else could have done to get me out. I had to trust God. What do you have to lose when you've tried everything else?

IDENTITY CRISIS

If I were to ask you who you are, what would you say? Do you know that who you are has nothing to do with the roles you perform? In today's world, it seems we are conditioned to derive our identity from our profession, our parenting, our education level, where we live, who we know, who knows us, what we look like, skin color, the house we live in, where we work, the car we drive, how much money we have in the bank, the church we attend and even who our significant other is...All things and people external to ourselves.

Take a minute to think of each of the abovementioned and the fleeting nature of each. Today, you can even change your physical features and skin color. None of these are unchangeable or immovable. As such, if our identity is to be based on any or many of these, it would make for a very unstable person. Yet, this is exactly what happens sometimes. Without the titles and the stuff, we have no idea who we are.

There will always be people who are richer, more liked, more educated, better dressed etc., then what? This is the part where some of us keep chasing the elusive dream only to be disappointed, empty and feeling as though who we are is never enough. There is a relentless competition to be more 'something' than the next person, or we are overly hard on ourselves to better, never being good enough right where we are.

NEWSFLASH:

Even if you were the best you could possibly be, there will always be someone better at doing what you do or who has more than you do. The great news is, with God, you are good enough right where you are. He never changes. He is who He says He is, and you are who He says you are.

Instead of constantly striving to be 'somebody,' we should be letting go or releasing everything to become a nobody, so that the power of Christ may rest on us. It's not that we can't have things or strive to excellence, but the things should not define who we are. We should only have one master.

BECOMING A NOBODY

We were all born with that innate desire to be loved and valued. We were created for purpose and to find fulfillment in walking that purpose out.

However, it was never God's intention that we figure it all out on our own or that our fulfillment would be found separate and apart from Him. I'm sure we've all discovered by now that we can't fill up on empty.

In fact, He created us for loving relationship with Him and wants us to walk in purpose even more than we want to. As such, He is more than willing and able to direct our steps and empower us to walk out the life story, He has already written.

We can't walk out our will and His will at the same time, but we can come to a place where His desires become our desires. It happens when we surrender our lives.

Context is important. This self-sacrificing can get unhealthy if in our minds, we are doing it unto a human being. When we understand that it is done unto God first, then it becomes an act of worship and pleasure unto God. Consequently, it is not predicated upon what the person does or doesn't do, but it is a choosing to lay down our lives for another out of love for God. The danger arises when we lay down our lives for the person for the sake of the person and that person is not who or what we expect or desire.

For whoever will save his life, shall lose it: and whosoever will lose his life for my sake shall find it. Matthew 16:25

It is in dying that we find ourselves…Unto God and not unto man.

In order for us to become one with God, self must die. It is in dying that we discover who we truly are…our identity. Likewise, in marriage, in order for two to become one, we must die to self while holding firm to our God-given identity.

Marriage is the relationship that God likens to the one He has with us, His bride, the Church.

'NO' IS A LOVE WORD

The word 'NO' has mostly been used to convey the negative, but when used appropriately, it can be very empowering.

I'm not sure when exactly it happened, but somewhere along the way, it was engrained in me that if I said 'No' to people in many scenarios that it was selfish of me. As a child, I was taught to share everything I had. As a woman, perhaps I was not told, but somehow saw it played out enough times to accept that we are to sacrifice ourselves for our husbands or significant others. Although, self-sacrifice in itself is not a bad thing and in the context of God's word, it is blessed, I believe that there is an aspect that we often neglect, and this renders our self-sacrifice to be unhealthy and oppressive, rather than blessed and freeing.

I speak here of ***'loving self'*** and knowing our identity.

> *Jesus said to him, "You shall love the* L*ORD your God with all your heart, with all your soul, and with all your mind. This is the first and great commandment. And the second is like it:* ***You shall love your neighbor as yourself.****" Matthew 22:37-39*

Loving my neighbour as myself means that I would not do to anyone what I would not want done to me. However, if I have an incorrect perception of self, can you see how that could be problematic? How we treat others would be different for different people based on what we believe about ourselves.

Although many use the term self-love, I'd like to be clear that it is my belief that if we don't have love, we can't give it to ***ourselves*** for we are not the originators or producers of love. God is the source of love, He is love and if we've never opened ourselves to receive His love, then we won't be full of it. Our love, human love is *self-ish* at best. God tells us in His Word what true love is, who we are to Him and what His thoughts and feelings are toward us. That does not change and it's not predicated on what we do or don't do.

If we don't have love, (the God kind of love), then we can't give it to others. If we don't know and understand who we are and more importantly whose we are, then we'll find ourselves in the position to be victimised. In essence, loving ourselves is more about knowing that we are loved and embracing and walking in that Love.

Loving self is not selfishness. Wait, I need to say that again:

LOVING SELF IS NOT SELFISHNESS!

When we understand that it's ok to love ourselves and to make decisions that serve us well, then we learn to appreciate the value and power of the word 'NO.' In fact, we may find ourselves using it very often in what we say and in what we don't say. Yes, there are some things that we don't need to verbally respond to, which in itself has a power all its own. You may be considered rude, but hey, let each one deal with oneself.

When we understand the love that God has for us and that He is all we need, we begin to come 'Out the Box' of 'people pleasing' and wanting to be liked by everyone. When we know our identity and how He sees us and thinks about us, we learn the power of 'No' and how to draw healthy boundaries for ourselves.

NEWSFLASH:

No matter what you do or how good you are, everyone is not going to like you, so you might as well live in full authenticity.

In fact, when you begin to live this way, you may find that you use the word 'No' more often and you no longer 'get along' with some people you used to get along with. There may be more people who get offended at you living your truth. The truth does offend as it rightfully should. Light exposes darkness. People have two choices when offended, and often, it is not personal. It usually happens because they see something in you that they want for themselves or become highly aware of what they don't like about themselves. Sometimes, truth is like a mirror being held up in front of us. We can use offence to make ourselves better, or we can hate on people and stay in our box.

We are not responsible for the reactions and feelings of others, but we are responsible for being who God created us to be.

Losing the 'love' of a man has been a catalyst in my receiving the greatest gift, LOVE. I've had a revelation of the never ending, unconditional love of God, and it has enabled me to grow into loving myself or rather, my God-identity or a 'knowing and being' loved. If I don't love and respect me, no one else will, but it comes from having an accurate perspective of how God sees me, and being secure in My relationship with Him. People will treat us the way we treat ourselves.

My Loving Self now says:

- "No, I won't permit you to treat me that way"
- "No, that decision is not right for me"
- "No, that is not God's will"
- "No, I won't enable you to continue in your dysfunction, addiction, irresponsibility…"
- "No, I won't save you because I love you"
- "No, your actions have consequences"
- "Of course, I forgive you, but NO, I won't permit you to do it to me again
- "No, I won't give up on my dreams/purpose for you"
- "I won't tell you YES because I'm afraid of how you'll react"
- "No, I won't allow you to control or manipulate me in the name of Christ Jesus. I know the Living WORD…, I know Him."

In conclusion, it is quite alright to say 'NO.' However, our NO does not necessarily need to be vocalised, but may be clearly articulated by our actions. When applied appropriately, 'NO' is certainly a Love word too.

Even God says 'No' to protect us from ourselves and to preserve us for His best. We must first understand His heart to gain perspective on His 'No.'

We sometimes deny ourselves by not denying ourselves, for God desires to gives us so much more than He may be asking us to let go.

The self-sacrifice of NO takes us deeper with Him. It crucifies our flesh. ***We are called to lose ourselves, but not our identity.***

God's No can work for the good of all involved. It can allow two people to build a rock-solid foundation.

Reflections:

1. Having you been saying Yes to people because you didn't want them to think you were selfish?
2. In making that decision, would you have had more inner peace in saying NO or saying YES?
3. What thought(s) stopped you from making the decision you wanted?
4. Think of an instance when you said YES, but really needed to say NO? How did it play out? What possibilities would saying NO have presented?
5. Are you prepared to face the consequences of saying NO?
6. Have you ever felt emotionally black mailed into saying YES?
7. How did it cause you to feel about (1) yourself and (2) the person?

NO MORE VICTIMS

When I started understanding how much God loved me and the person He created me to be, I started to live from that place.

As I began to live on purpose and be intentional about my choices, it empowered me. I understood that I could respond how I wanted to and not react to stimuli.

I learnt the power of silence and the power of the word 'NO.' I didn't have to say 'yes' to people out of fear that they would not like me, or that they would no longer 'do' something for me. For, I now know who my SOURCE is, and that with Him, nothing is impossible to me.

I believe that if we are aware of what someone is actually doing and we see it, and choose how we want to respond, then we are no longer operating as victims. It's all about our free will and power of CHOICE.

GODFIDENCE

I don't consider myself to be a self-confident person. In fact, there are many things I would never do on my own if it weren't for the Lord.

What I do have is God confidence. I believe that if He has asked me to do it, then He will empower me to be able to. In fact, He has already given me the potential to do it, hidden to be revealed. If He has brought me to it, I've been prepared for it already. If He believes I can do it and trusts me to, who am I to say I can't?

With Him, nothing shall be impossible to me.

I step out in boldness because I know He's with me and He loves me. If God is for me, who can be against? So, when He speaks, I step out in Godfidence.

Our perception of others and ourselves can cause us to operate from a place of fear, and thus beneath where God designed for us to operate.

I had a scenario where I felt intimidated because in my mind, the other people in this meeting were very professional and knew more than I did.

I hesitated to give my contribution, but in doing so, there was much value. What I shared was important in making a final determination on a matter.

Often the enemy will bring fear to cripple us or stop our purpose actions. The best way to deal with fear is to face it head on, and do that thing anyway.

God has already said that He has not given me a spirit of fear but of power, love and soundness of mind. 2 Timothy 1:7. I have to know this. In other words, I have to believe, trust and act as though He is as His word says. When I know Him, then shall I do 'great exploits.'

I recognise that it's not always in what we actually say or how we say it, but in saying it with the anointing of God that makes it impactful.

I can get caught up in myself and miss the opportunity to show up for God in the lives of others. Self-focus causes me to function from a place of fear, but faith-focus causes me to transcend my feelings and what I see currently. I must know that if He's sent me to speak that in my yielding, He'll speak through me.

"And my speech and preaching were not with persuasive words of human wisdom, but in demonstration of the Spirit and of power." 1 Corinthians 2:4

There's a strength that comes from knowing that we are in God's will. There is a boldness and a fearlessness like when you walk into a space with d 'Boss-man.' When you've been in a place where you couldn't trust anyone but God, and He comes through for you, you know it's not by your power. That's how you get Godfidence.

"I can do all things through Christ who strengthens me." Philippians 4:13

**'Godfidence' is available in a T-shirt.*

BEAUTIFUL SCARS

My scars make me beautiful.
They remind me of where He brought me from
And though, they hurt no more
They're the reason why I soar.
Misunderstood, abused and rejected
All the while,
My God protected me from losing my mind
Despite their words and deeds unkind.
Where would I have been
Had He not intervened?
Thinking I knew it all, yet,
Heading for a great fall-
Ing into loving arms outstretched
Many things I could regret
But thankful my story wasn't done
My heart He stole, He won.
And now, I have hope
I can dream again, and
I can do things I'd never thought possible.
By His embrace I'm hidden and safe
Lifted to a secret place
With a vantage point of flight
Where I overcome,
Not by my power or might
Where I trust Him and
Live by faith not sight.

THE HOUSE IN THE VALLEY

I lived in our 'dream house' after we were divorced and spent six months there. We were divorcing while it was being built. Soon after moving to the house that was being renovated in the east, he moved up to the house in the valley and left me there. In terms of our settlement, I had a deadline by which I had to vacate the east house. I stayed beyond that date because I was given grace.

My ex-husband-to be (as I called him) had suggested that I move up to help settle our son who had just switched schools. I had left my job at an educational institution months before, and I took the opportunity to finally finish my Life Coaching Programme. That's where I learnt submission because it was like I was 'begging a lodging.' I was really in his house…he bought me out in our settlement.

Left up to me alone, I probably would have never done this, but I knew that this was Daddy's wish. Who wants to live with their ex after they've been divorced? He had a conversation with me about how I would feel if 'his friend' came over. I said to him that I would never disrespect him in his home. I would be mannerly, but that she would never be my friend.

I made the move. One of the things about my living there was that he didn't have to give me any money for our son. No issue there…it's not as though I wasn't using it to take care of him. For the most part, we lived like roommates and co-parented. Everything was common except our bedrooms and bathrooms. Sometimes, he ate when I cooked, but I was under no obligation to cook for him or do anything else. As long as

I was in the house, none of his female friends came there. When I'd left for the weekend was another story.

This was not the kind of place where people who lived there walked or took public transport to get where they were going, but I did, rain or shine. I found out later from one of the neighbours that he'd said that we were trying again, but that was not our arrangement. That did not stop him from *'pulling at'* me (making advances) though.

I couldn't believe that he expected me to take him seriously when he was still with her, or rather when she thought that they were together. In as much as I was shown no respect, I respected other people's relationships. I would not do to another woman what I didn't want for myself. Many years prior, perhaps, but not at that stage of my life.

I'm sure that people assumed that once we were living together that we were having sex. That was so far from the truth, and it became increasingly frustrating for us both. For him because I was rejecting his advances, and for me because they were being made.

I didn't just want a man, I wanted a husband. As far as I was concerned, we weren't married (although we were), and God told me that he would be a new creature in Christ, so I was waiting for that new creature to appear.

He said to me once that he hoped I didn't have it in my head that we would reconcile and even if he wound up in a wheelchair, he would never accept Christ. The things we say...I felt scared for him when he said that. He was such a proud man, and I know God has a way of humbling us.

Let me say that I'm not superwoman, nor was I frigid, but I was not about sex for the sake of sex. I didn't need to have sex to feel loved or to validate who I am (different life stage).

I wanted emotional and spiritual connection. I also wanted to honour God, and besides, I don't share. I said to God that if he expected me to abstain, He needed to take away the desire and urges from me until it was time for them. He was faithful, so it wasn't much of a struggle. What I craved and missed were intimacy and companionship. I've had many, many lonely nights.

I've lived in the big houses, and I've had a lot of stuff in my life, but I was still lonely and unfulfilled in my marriage. I've always wanted a happy marriage. I would have traded some of the stuff and the lifestyle any day just for a loving relationship. During those lonely times and throughout the painful processing, the Lord gave me Isaiah 54:

> *Fear not, for you shall not be ashamed, neither be confounded, for you shall not be put to shame: for you shall forget the shame of your youth and shall not remember the reproach of thy widowhood any more.*
> *For your Maker is your husband, the Lord of Hosts is His name and your Redeemer, the Holy One of Israel, the God of the whole earth shall He be called.*
> *For the Lord has called you as a woman forsaken and grieved in spirit, and a wife of youth when you were refused, says your God…*
> *For a mere moment I have forsaken you, but with great mercies I will gather you. With a little wrath I hid My face from you for a moment; But with everlasting kindness I will have mercy on you…" Verses 4-8*

I did not hate my ex-husband-to be. I actually did love him, but I didn't feel the romantic kind of love (Eros). What I felt went way beyond that I think. A relationship can change a lot in six months if you're open to it though. I think we had gotten to a place of forgiveness and even friendship.

THE DEPARTURE

One of the times when I heard the Lord so clearly, it was almost audible, he said to me, "You know you're going to have to leave Chilo, right?" I would have doubted, except it was so clear, and I would never have come up with that.

Just to make sure, by the next day, two other people would have said it to me. One of them, saw it in a vision that I was visiting my son, and he was not living with me. I confirmed to her that she saw right because Daddy had already told me. So, I settled in my heart, as painful as it was that it would be as the Lord said.

About a week later, Mr. Ex-To Be came up with a grand proposition. He cited that he couldn't continue living the way we were because he's a man, and I was not with him and it's frustrating. My options were to either move to the basement and pay him a rent or move out. Whatever my decision, our son would be staying with him. I already knew what my answer was to be because God had already told me, but I told him that I would give him my answer by the end of the week.

The intention behind this was to still be in a position to exercise control over me, to have his cake and eat it too. He would either have a live-in babysitter when he brought women to the house, and he could send Chilo downstairs, and get paid too, or he would get me back. He thought that I would never have left Chilo with him. Moving him to school in Port of Spain was also a part of that plan in hindsight, but that worked for Chilo's good and his. He became a better man for it.

At the end of the week, I advised him that I had decided to leave. He seemed quite shocked, but could say nothing else at that point, but "Okay." I got the truck and moved, yet again back to my parents' home in south.

I had paid down on a townhouse with my cash from my settlement, and wound up without house or money. I had to take legal action and to this day, I still haven't gotten back all of it. I am thankful for what I have gotten back though, and I'm still receiving payments. It always comes at the right time. I have no doubt that it will all come back to me though…even if it's not from that source.

I had our son almost every weekend. It became automatic. Our original arrangement by court order was supposed to be, I was to have care and control, and we each had to give at least one day's notice as it related to where he was going to be. I had already relinquished care and control, and I welcomed any opportunity to have him.

God really knows best, and I love that He brought comfort to my heart. I remember reading something shortly after I had left Chilo in the valley that talked about how at a certain age, there is a shift from mom that needs to happen and a deeper connection to their father that needs to be formed for the proper development of boys. Chilo was just about that age.

THE ISSUE OF BLOOD

Chilo spent two years 'in the valley.' During that time, his dad and I had actually become friends, and we went out a lot with him and a few times without him.

I had no expectations of him because I knew that any transformation or reconciliation was in God's hands. Much of the time, I couldn't fully be myself, because I knew that wouldn't have made for the smoothest of interactions, but I listened to him and I asked many questions.

We were able to talk about things that we were never able to in our marriage and in a way that was not possible before. Prayer changes things, and God had done a lot of healing in our relationship. We came to the point where apart from re-marriage, we had reconciled.

He never stopped showing interest though, and when it seemed as though things were starting to go somewhere, he reconnected with someone. I knew this by the change in his attitude toward me and his trying to fight down the Jesus in me. I made a decision at that time that I was not going to spend time with him or go out with him anymore. It didn't make sense, and I said to God, whatever you want to do, do it and let me know, but I'm done. That was November 2013

I wondered whether He had released me too because a friend had messaged me from the States to say that she had a dream. She saw me standing at a crossroads waiting, and I was getting very tired of waiting.

My own dreams had shifted as well. Instead of seeing us all together, I was dreaming that only Chilo and I were going on a plane together, or we were in a different country.

In one of the dreams, I was at the gate and trying to figure out how come we were there, and I couldn't remember having my passport. I was trying to go back and search for it. When I got up, the Lord was saying that He had already made the way for me to go, and that all was well.

In reality, the three of us had gone to renew passports for Chilo and me. I changed names on mine, reverting to my maiden name. Our current passports were expiring in August and September and our US Visas were in those.

In another dream, Mr. Ex-To-Be and I were in what seemed to be an apartment or hotel room. Two ladies came to talk to him, one of East Indian and one of African descent. The strange thing was, he was lying in the bed and was not getting up. So, I took what seemed to be their business cards from them. This dream would prove its meaning in weeks to come.

In reality, I had gone to the bank to transact some business and I was told that the 'I Do' account that we had opened when we had gotten married, should not have still been open. We had kept it as a joint account to deal with deposits for Chilo. I had spoken to him about closing it and opening an account for Chilo.

He said to me that he would deal with it in July after he had taken his CFA exams. (This never happened) This was the third or fourth time that he was taking this level.

I had met someone as well. This was significant because it was as though the Lord had me in a cocoon for years and I was invisible. I was also, not available. Now, it seemed as though I was visible again. As a friend called to say, "The Lord says that the hedge is removed."

Things never really progressed with this person, although I believe we both cared for each other, but I see the reasons for why we didn't move forward to be all God's orchestration, and for our best.

Somewhere around March 2014, I had a dream that Mr. Ex-To-Be came to me, and his body bore deep, open wounds with maggots falling out of them. I didn't say much to him and he went and sat down under an old house (resembling his grandfather's house I had seen in a picture). A relative then came to me and said, "Jilean, that's it, he's gone." In the dream, I was saying, "OMG, and he came to me and I didn't say anything to him."

This dream really concerned me, and I asked the Lord whether I should say anything to him. I was released to do so. I said to him, "Whatever wounds or hurts you have, you need to deal with them or it will eat you alive from the inside out." He said that he wasn't concerned because it was my dream and not his.

About a week later, he said to me that his wounds are that he feels that no matter what he has done or how much he's accomplished in his life, he feels that in his loved ones' eyes, he's done nothing because it's not in the name of Jesus.

He felt that we had all ostracised him because he was not following Jesus. I said to him that we all knew where he stood, and we knew not to tell him anything, but obviously people of like-mind would gravitate to each other. I asked, "Have you ever thought that you are the person that has been pushing us away?"

On Easter Monday 2014, Mr. Ex-To-Be said to me that he was ready to do whatever it took for us to be in a committed relationship and to be a family again, but Jesus is not his path. My response was that God would never force his will, even though He's given a word. If this was his choice, then I had to say that there can't be any 'us.'

The next time I saw him, I did notice that he'd lost a lot of weight, but I thought that he was exercising intensely. In May, sometime after Mothers' Day, I was at a function, and he Whatsapped me saying, "I haven't been feeling well. Feels like I'm dying. The doctor says I should not be driving, so I need you to come up, so we can go for Chilo and carry the results for the Haematologist."

Needless to say, I left the function, went home to pack up some clothes and travelled to his Port of Spain Office to meet him. He had on a jacket because he said he'd been cold sweating. We passed for Chilo in school and proceeded to the Blood Specialist. She said that he either had an extreme form of Anemia or he had Leukemia, but either way, he needed an immediate blood transfusion or his organs would begin to shut down. We were to go to the POS General Hospital the next day to get the transfusion.

Later that evening, he gave me telephone and internet access to his accounts. It's a good thing that we never closed the joint account because this is how I was able to transfer funds and do all that was needed. To think that he was trying to withhold money from me a few years prior...

Even in his illness, I saw the grace of God. God is indeed merciful. He gave him a chance to repent and change his heart. The doctor said, they have seen people dropping down with better blood test results, and he was amazed that he was still walking around. What if he had knocked out while driving to south with Chilo?

The next day at the hospital, the doctor said that the results from the CBC looked like Leukemia. They actually drew more blood. It was painful to watch as they barely got any. To make matters worse, they had to do it again because the first batch was compromised.

My husband was eventually diagnosed with Acute Myeloid Leukemia. Interestingly, when the reality of it sank in, he said, "Leukemia, I rejected His blood, so He's taking it back." How profound a statement...

The statement was an acknowledgement for me of who he knew God was, yet he did not bow his knees at that point. That was to happen many weeks ahead...

We never had to beg for blood donors. He was just given the blood he needed. They put him in a separate room by himself because of his low immunity level. There was no way that he was leaving the hospital that day like he thought, so I had to go pack clothes to bring back for him.

I spent that week back and forth from the valley house to the hospital, the bank, the Haematologist, Chilo's school and wherever else. I was exhausted. I had really great friends, some I didn't know I had who helped with Chilo, making sure we ate and supported us in immeasurable ways. Let me say here, thank you, you know who you are.

He had a bone marrow aspirate done to send to the lab for testing. They could barely find a sample to test. The results concluded Acute Myeloid Leukemia. The doctor said to him that this was very aggressive, but not treated in Trinidad. If at all he could go abroad, he should have left yesterday. He spent one week exactly in the hospital during which time, he told everyone that I was his wife.

My 'husband' was discharged on a Friday, and the next day, he was on a plane to the US. A dear mutual friend of ours had agreed to go to the US with him, while I stayed back to put some things in place before leaving. As it turned out, the dream about him on the bed unable to move was him being in the hospital unable to transact business. The ladies in the dream were the two tenants who he later asked me to collect rent from on his behalf.

Twice, I was asked over the previous two years whether he should sell the valley house, to which I responded in the negative. I felt that Chilo had just settled down and I wanted some stability for him. In his now sixteen years, that child has moved seven times. I've lost count how many times I've moved.

Selling the house would mean upheaval and relocation again, in addition to going through the construction of yet another house. He still decided to sell the house and it was in mid-sale when we learnt of his condition.

One of the things I needed to organise before leaving Trinidad was to have the house packed up for a relative to move everything out while I was gone. We had no house to come back to. I would only understand his motivation for still selling the house in 2018, four years after his death.

I took Chilo out of school early to go to the USA with me. Just as in my dream, the ticket was bought, and my passport was in order. How it played out is that I had to leave the new passport inside and travel with the old one that had my married name, otherwise, I would have had to reapply for a US visa.

Also, there was a relax on the requirement to have at least six months' validity on passports for travel to the States. When I got to the States, my passport was still stamped for six months even though it expired in less than three.

My brother lived in New York at the time, so I stayed with him on Staten Island and did the trains and ferries back and forth from the hospital almost every day. There were a few days missed. One of the reasons was I got the flu while I was there, and I could not visit.

Initially, I was juicing fruit and vegetable blends for Leukemia and taking for him, but he said that he didn't like how he was feeling when he drank it. I think it was probably doing something positive, but I stopped at his request. It amazed me how they don't feed people life giving foods in cancer hospitals and wards, especially since all the medications are depleting and not replenishing, but that's a whole other story.

My 'husband' underwent chemotherapy in the first hospital, came out for a week and went into a State hospital where he did another round of chemo. He got favour in the second hospital. He had a great view in his own room with an extra bed in the room for me.

During the week that he was out, he wanted to do things with Chilo and me. We went to movies, Ripley's Believe It or Not, he took the ferry across to Staten Island. He was not always the easiest person to be around, but who can fault anyone who is facing mortality for being a bit less than chipper?

I was given very specific words from God about this journey and the outcome, but one thing trumped all for me. God said that he would be a new creature in Christ and until that happened, he wasn't going anywhere. So, this is how I prayed because this is what it was all about, a soul who God loved and wanted to save.

What do you say to someone who asks you, "Do you believe I'm going to live?" Well, my answer was, "You'll live if you want to live." He responded, "Why you can't just give a simple answer?" The question was quite a weighty one.

We can do all the things in life we know to stay healthy and still be faced with illness. It is only by the grace of God we live. I saw nurses coming to his bedside constantly to check his vitals, stick him for blood etc., he had no rest. Walking through this journey with him opened my eyes to so many simple blessings we take for granted every day...family and friends who love us, the human touch-skin to skin, our own warm bed, hot water, uninterrupted sleep, the ability to speak and communicate, taking a shower and using the washroom on our own, walking, to name just a few. Imagine your world tomorrow without any one of these? Now, imagine his world without all, but one, family and friends who loved him.

My husband developed a critical infection from the overgrowth of a bacterium called C Diff. We all have it in our gut, but it doesn't affect us negatively because we have a functioning immune system. This bacterium was eating away at his stomach from the inside out, and it was very painful for him. One of his nurses, after observing him over two days did not like what she was seeing and escalated for him to be sent to the ICU.

When he arrived at the ICU, he was so insistent that I call back the nurse who made the call to bring him down. He wanted to tell her thank you. Up until that point, his pride was so much in play. This gesture smelt only of humility. Something had changed in his heart.

The doctors decided to open him up to see whether his gut was dying and whether they could cut out any problematic parts. They cautioned that they didn't know what they would find, or 'what would happen.'

In other words, they didn't know whether he'd survive the surgery. They also wanted to leave him open to administer the medication directly to the source and go back in the next day.

I did not make this decision alone, but contacted a relative and had the doctors speak to us both. He agreed and the surgery was performed. Before going in for the surgery, I said to my husband, "Know that I love you, I forgive you, and you have nothing to worry about. Now put your life in the hands of the Lord, you can't do anything to save yourself now, can you?" He shook his head, as if to say, "Is true." "I'll see you soon ok," said I.

The surgery was performed, and he did come out of it, but they would never take out the tubes from his throat, and he would never speak audibly to us again. His mind was sharp to the end though.

The doctors told everyone (with him present) later that evening that they didn't know if his heart would hold out. They wanted to know whether they should try to resuscitate or not. He wouldn't answer, so it was left alone. A pastor was called that evening to pray with him and in the presence of us all, my husband surrendered all of his life to Jesus as Lord and Saviour, by a shaking of his head.

God would not let the prayers of his saints go in vain. At the beginning of this journey, I knew that it was only between him and God.

I stayed after everyone had left. It was after midnight, and by then, I'd been in the hospital for forty-eight hours. My brother came over from Staten Island with Chilo to the hospital. He had been preparing him for that late-night trip. I didn't want to be going home to tell our son that his Daddy died without him having the opportunity to see him and say goodbye. He hadn't been going to the hospital anymore because he didn't want to see his Dad with all the tubes, but he agreed to see him that night after I explained to him that things were uncertain.

Father and son saw each other for the last time with a visit that ended with Chilo saying, "Bye Daddy." Chilo was ten, Daddy was forty-seven. I'll end now by saying that my husband died at around four a.m. I was by his side until they called a 'Code Blue' and rushed in, putting me out of the room. I could still see what was happening. I'd never imagined that process to be so violent, but it is the image that remained in my mind for some time. This is what traumatised me, and I was hoping that he had already left his body when that was being done. It's not a peaceful way to go.

His family handled the funeral arrangements, but when we returned to Trinidad, the support we received was overwhelming. Friends offered their vehicles for us to move around and get things done. Chilo and I had to move to our north apartment. Thankfully, the furniture had already been moved in. Books and uniform needed to be sorted for the return to school in a couple weeks.

Tribute to My Husband

There's no way for your life to have crossed paths with My Husband without it having been changed in some way. For me, knowing him has ultimately catapulted me into a place of purpose and meaning. For that, I am forever thankful.

This journey has not always been pleasant because boy could he push my buttons, but it challenged me to become a better person, it strengthened my faith in God and most importantly, it taught me to see into the heart of God and how merciful and loving He is.

Many of you expressed shock at his passing. You said things like, "He was so fit, he ate well, he exercised, he was so young..." Yes, these are all true, but what God permitted is a reminder to us all that our lives are not our own and that it is purely by the grace of God that we have breath.

Thank you for all your prayers and support through this journey. Many of us believed for a miracle or healing... I want to let you know that the greatest miracle occurred when he surrendered his life to The Lord Jesus Christ before his departure from this world. So, in the midst of the pain and sorrow which is natural when someone we love is no longer with us, there is also peace and there is much joy in heaven.

The word of God says in Mark 9:45-47" ...It is better for you to enter life lame, than, having your two feet, to be cast into hell, [where THEIR WORM DOES NOT DIE, AND THE FIRE IS NOT QUENCHED.] "If your eye causes you to stumble, throw it out; it is better for you to enter the kingdom of God with one eye, than, having two eyes, to be cast into hell." It is this word that helps me to make some sense of things and to have comfort, for I know that he, though not whole in body at the end of his earthly days will spend an eternity with the Lord.

His life was a gift to us from God. Let his journey not be in vain. Perhaps, we will now re-evaluate and re-prioritize what is really important. Maybe, we will cherish those around us a bit more, and nurture our relationships with those we love, for we only have today, and life can change so drastically in an instant. May we seek the joy of The Lord and surrender our lives to Him while we still have time, for tomorrow is promised to none of us.

He was my friend, my husband, my ex-husband, the father of our son, and a host of other titles, but he was a man that The Lord used to teach me how to love as He does. He was a man through whom the Lord showed me the lengths He would go to win our hearts.

Husband, I love you and you will never be forgotten. I will ever be reminded of you, as I see your distinct qualities in our son, Chilo. You will live on through him in both our hearts. Thanks for sharing your life with us. I know we will see you again someday.

NOTES FROM A REPENTANT HUSBAND

After my husband died, I'd said to the Lord that I'd wished I had known how he really felt about me. He did say he loved me, but I wanted more insight into where his head and heart were.

A few months later, I was going through some books, and I came across a note pad he was scribbling on while he studied. My Father never ceases to amaze me…the prayers He answers. My deceased husband's words brought tears to my eyes…

The following is what he wrote:

Jilean, a sweet and gentle flower.
Changes I know there are many, but my love for you remains constant.
I understand your hurt, your pain and hesitation- I would be the same. Most in my mind are thoughts of making it right. To be right by you. Not forgiveness, but erasure. Closure!
I cried like a baby in your arms. You held me and, in your embrace, I felt loved, comforted and at home.

I've strayed, walked too far -distant in the horizon, the edge where I fall into a seemingly endless freefall into emptiness.
Bring me back Oh God! And keep me, and make me who you want me to be!

Am I losing my mind?
How do I find
To open my eyes to see, to look, to seek, to recapture
Sometimes I am in a swirl

Round and round in a twirl
Being played by someone else's fingers.

Trying to study, but my mind is jumping from one thought to the next...can't seem to focus.

A WIDOW'S LETTER

In the last year, I've had many revelations about events and conversations that transpired between me and my deceased husband.

It caused me to wonder, just when are we ever ready to 'move on?' It has taken so many years to get to this point. I now find myself in this place where I'm understanding the dynamics of our past interactions and where his heart was with things.

I'm writing this letter as my closure to this chapter of my life, and I look forward with great anticipation to my NEW husband, armed with the wisdom and love I've grown into.

Dear Husband

Who would have known that there'd still be things I would want to say to you after you've been gone for four years?

They say hindsight is 20-20 vision. I now see what I couldn't then. I wonder why Daddy didn't show me before…perhaps, He tried and I just wasn't in the place to see.

I'm not sure whether you have a vantage point of our lives now. Should you be so graced, I'm certain there are things you would be proud of. Also, in earthly, human terms, some things would otherwise have concerned you. So amazing for you though, you're with the Lord, and you know that no matter how things look now, He's got us and we'll be fine.

Here are the things I'd like to say:

1. I understand now how frustrating it must have been for you because I didn't see the Religious System or Church Matrix for what it is. I understand now that you were just trying to live in freedom and not be entangled again in bondage.

   Now, I see the heart condition you were living with, but you threw out Jesus with the bath water. It's sad that He has been so misrepresented for so long...

   We all need Him, not just as Saviour, but as Lord. It is in letting go of ourselves and relinquishing control of our lives to Him that we find ourselves. It is bitter-sweet that you got this at the end of your earthly life

2. I see now that you wanted me to pursue my destiny and be a whole me, even though you were ill equipped to husband me into that place. This is what you meant when you said, "Just do you and I'll do me." The responsibility of making me happy was too heavy a burden for you or anyone to carry. Especially, when we had our own brokenness to deal with

3. I understand now about why you still sold the "House in the Valley." You felt ashamed of its history, your history with the women. Your friend told me after you died that you had plans of remarrying me that December. You wanted a fresh start for all of us. That's why you were buying the piece of land to build again. I couldn't understand why you'd want to go through all that again, but now, I do

4. You were an extraordinary man, and way ahead of your time in many ways. Had we both been healed and totally surrendered to His leading, we would have been a powerful union in the earth

5. You were a great Dad and you had a vision for your family. Thank you for thinking ahead, even though things didn't quite work out as you had planned

6. I guess you understand now why I could not reconcile in the way you'd liked. I loved you in a way you could not comprehend at the time. You could not have my hand again without coming to my Father. Losing me meant you gained Him.

I could not 'move on' until you were His. I'm glad
that Daddy didn't allow me to do what I wanted, when I wanted. The sacrifice treated with my heart condition. It also protected me from myself.

Thank you for all the richness and depth you brought to my life, whether directly or indirectly. My life is better for having had you in it, and Daddy has worked all things together for my good.

See you later…

Jilean

FAITH, FEAR AND LOVE

Is protecting oneself for fear of disappointment or hurt a lack of trust? Furthermore, is it sin?

"...whatever is not from faith is sin..." Romans 14:23

Faith in God comes from love, knowledge and intimacy. If I know Him, I'll trust Him even when what I see doesn't make sense or seems contrary.

"Love bears all things, believes all things, hopes all things." Corinthians 13:7

God wants to fill us to capacity and overflowing with His love so that we would be satisfied and have more than enough to share, for we can't give what we don't have. In order to have, we must be willing to open all the chambers of our hearts to Him.

...that Christ may dwell in your hearts through faith; that you, being rooted and grounded in love, may be able to comprehend with all the saints what is the width and length and depth and height to know the love of Christ which passes knowledge; that you may be filled with the fullness of God. Ephesians 3:17-18

He doesn't give His heart in pieces, He gave and continues to give us His all...

Have you ever been in love with someone, but couldn't be with that person? Having to hold back can be torturous. It's been a painful thing to love God with pieces of my heart (or closed chambers), although I wasn't always aware that this was the cause of some of my distress.

Why do we hold back pieces? It's either because of fear or we just don't know that we have chambers of our hearts that are closed to Him. Either way, we need His love to free us and open our hearts up. Sometimes, this love comes tough, and it breaks open our hearts, but His love is perfect, and it never fails.

We cannot be in fear and love at the same time. We are usually acting out from one place or the other.

"There is no fear in love; but perfect love casts out fear, because fear involves torment. But he who fears has not been made perfect in love. We love Him because He first loved us." I John 4:18-19

SAVING IS NOT ALWAYS HELPING

There are some situations over which we have no control, but there are many over which we do. We often have a blind spot when it comes to certain situations that are close to our hearts as to how our actions could be contributing to the perpetuation of our own drama.

We aid and abet people in continuing to have unhealthy relationships with themselves and others when we fail to allow them the gift of standing the consequences of their actions. It is a mistake to keep rescuing others who don't think they need help or who don't want to be rescued. For some, many a life lesson is learnt the 'hard way' or through experience, trials and pain.

We don't change until we get uncomfortable where we are. None of us would like to see our relatives suffering, going to jail, out on the street, hurting, but sometimes, this is necessary for them to hit rock bottom and get to the place where they realise they need the Saviour. Many strongholds in our lives present as addiction, although we often attribute addiction to substance abuse.

Just as an addict needs to be able to acknowledge there is a problem and want to change, the same holds true for many other life scenarios- gambling, lust, sex, infidelity, all forms of abuse, unhealthy relationships, poverty, poor money management, among others. Apart from prayer and faith, there are practical steps that need to be taken in order for deliverance to occur. The supply of whatever a person's habit feeds on needs to be cut off (a form of fasting). It may be physical or material, as well as emotional.

When we bail people out of situations they have found themselves in which more often than not affect the rest of the family or workplace, it may seem to fix the situation, but it will only do so temporarily. We cannot deny others the opportunity for growth and freedom by sparing them the consequences of their poor choices. There is priceless learning material in the pit, but our pulling them out short circuits their growth process and causes the cycle of dysfunction to continue. Then, we find ourselves saying things like, "I've done everything to help him, but he continues to...," throwing pity parties and complaining to others about what *so and so* is doing, rather than examining our role in contributing to the problem.

You may not understand all the intricacies of a scenario, but if you want different, you have to **do** different. Try to determine the root and the source of nourishment. Ask God to show you what the problem is, if you have been unintentionally contributing, and what you can do differently. God knows everything. Be willing to obey, even if it doesn't come naturally or may feel uncomfortable. Even new shoes are a bit uncomfortable until they get broken in.

Our lack of *loving self* or I prefer to say not knowing our identity often prevents us from saying 'No' or doing what God is instructing us to do because we don't want to run the risk of others thinking we are selfish or unloving...this thinking is fear-based. It is valuing the love, opinions and approval of people more than we do the love and approval of God. This in itself can be a form of addiction, as it can have so much control over every area of our lives.

We can have a dependency on having the approval of others that it causes us to continue feeding the addictions and dysfunction of those around us. Then, we can talk about how much we've done for them and how 'good' we've been and glorify ourselves at their expense. Unfortunately, many a sense of self-worth is derived through the unhealthy dependency of others on us as it can evoke a feeling of being 'needed.'

There is always a price we pay for this however, and the same holds true whether we believe the devil is real or figurative, as he will always take as much room as we give him. We give him room in our lives when we operate in fear instead of faith, and by extension in the lives of those we love and genuinely want to help because we fail to do 'the God instructed thing.' We will reap what we sow.

We are in error as long as we are trying to get our self-worth and feeling of being loved and fulfilled from any source other than God, as no one and nothing can fill that void but Him. Our failure to take 'right action' is the selfish thing to do because it attempts to show love in a way that is self-serving (not always consciously) under the guise of helping the other person. When, in fact, it serves no one well, not us, or the persons involved, both remain imprisoned 'in the box.'

THE BLESSING OF DRAMA

We like to say that we're 'blessed to be a blessing,' but do we really understand what that means? Did we ever think that our blessing would come in the form of hardship? I know I never used to…

I see it so clearly now. I wouldn't be here writing this book if I hadn't gone through the things I had. At the time I was in the throes of drama and pain, I couldn't see that these 'goings on' in my life were birthing purpose. They were developing character and bestowing wisdom on me.

I cannot deny that sometimes, "***wisdom comes from having done foolish things***," but God liberally gives us wisdom when we ask, and one of the ways we get it is through pain, struggle and trial.

No child is born into this world without the pain of labour. In the natural scheme of things, we must push through pain, and that child passes through a very narrow passage and comes out of a hidden space to be revealed to the wide world. We don't really focus on the pain after the child is born.

As I type this, I'm transported to a time when there were some exceptions though, some disappointments, some bitter-sweet experiences. There were a couple times when I did carry babies who did not go to full term. I'm remembering the two children that I'd lost, one in the second trimester and one in the first. It is only recently that I've thought about seeing my babies in heaven, the ones I never had a chance to meet.

Prior to now, I'd just thought of them as lost, and never held a hope of one day meeting the souls that were once assigned to me. I'm not sure why I had never thought about this until now.

On both occasions, my conception was a surprise. In one instance, I was on the pill. Given that I was experiencing so much unhappiness and stress in my marriage, initially, I was not pleased about these pregnancies. I told the doctor that I didn't want to be pregnant, but that I don't think God would approve. He said to me that if I had that conviction, then he won't have any part in aborting.

I eventually accepted these pregnancies as God's will because He alone is the giver of life. I thought of all the women who had been trying to conceive with no success. I thought of how I was barely getting pregnant myself, given my history of polycystic ovaries and endometriosis.

In the case of the baby I'd lost in the second trimester, he or she died inside of me and spent close to two weeks inside. One could say that I happened to go to the doctor on a visit here and the discovery was made, but nothing happens by chance. It was around the time when I should have been feeling movement, and I was getting very excited. An ultrasound would show no heartbeat...

Without giving a ball by ball account, I was prescribed pills to induce labour, and I went into the hospital and 'had my baby.' Yes, labour was very painful, but there was no baby at the end of it. Was this labour in vain? Only God knows. There was a part of me that felt that He knew that I could not handle another child at that point in time, so I consoled myself with that. I did still mourn, but not for very long. Perhaps, this pain would have been much worse had we not already had a son or if our marriage was a happy one. The irony of it all is that

I had our first son via Caesarean section, but I had this child 'the normal way.'

The week after this birthing ordeal, I was contacted by an insurance agent about increasing my life insurance coverage. He was telling me that I would need to have a medical done. Really? He was advised to do so by my husband who recognised how fickle life was and that I could have died from poisoning. At the time, I thought nothing could have been more insensitive or sinister. Long story short, this never happened.

Believe it or not, I have held this fantasy of having a daughter (I'm told girls are different) with the new husband (well, now I know his name is Errol). I've wanted to experience what pregnancy would be like with a man who truly loves and cherishes me. What would it be like to be spoiled and pampered? As long as my husband desires to have a child, it is my desire to have his child. It would be an honour.

In the past, I'd been told things like, "What happen? Don't expect any special treatment you know. You're only pregnant, women do it all the time," or "You not really made for babies you know."

In addition, my parents have no granddaughters. I've told my Dad that he needs to stay alive to see his granddaughter. In the natural, it seems impossible now, but I've spoken this child into being for years, and I know that with God, all things are possible. We'll see...His will be done.

Coming out of the pain of emotional abuse, baby loss and divorce, Women Out the Box was birthed. Women Out the Box is a private group on Facebook which provides a safe space for women to share, receive support, gain freedom and be empowered to walk in purpose. It is about coming out of the boxes of limitation in which we either placed ourselves or allowed others to place us.

Suffering in silence without an outlet or person to talk to would no longer be the only option if I could do something about it. Women Out the Box is a space I also needed, and as Jill came 'out the box,' she would help other women to do the same, with God's help of course. In 2019, we celebrated 10 years of existence.

Important to note is the fact that over the years, there were many times when I felt like I was in that space by myself, talking to the wind- there were no likes or comments. Was it discouraging at times? Certainly, but my motive kept me going.

I wasn't doing it for likes and interaction, I was doing it because I believe I was led by God to, and I wanted to help other women get free. I didn't need to 'see,' to continue doing what He wanted me to, I did it by faith. I think Father also wanted my faith to be in Him only, so He permitted it to be that I wouldn't always get feedback or interaction because it couldn't be about me.

God did allow me at different points though to know that people were in fact reading and being helped because when they saw me, they'd tell me that they read and encourage me to keep writing. The thing I'm trying to get at here is that motive is important…we must know why we are doing what we are. That's the difference between persevering and giving up.

In 2018, Women Out the Box jumped out of the virtual box to the reality of meeting in person. Our next meeting will be our fifth. I didn't know it at inception, but this was the birthing of 'a ministry,' a movement and would be the avenue through which my first Coaching clients came.

BE FIRST...

Stay focused on becoming the person God created you to be, and your God-ordained spouse will find you. **We must become before he or she comes.** God won't give us His best to spoil it.

God will present you to your spouse. You need not go looking or trying to position yourself. Just keep pursuing purpose and becoming your best self. In order to attract a king or queen, one must first become regal.

Sometimes, that is a painful journey or process as God dredges up deep sediments and residual junk in preparing us for His stage. We don't always see the point of the waiting or the time in between when we think we're ready, but God knows exactly what He's doing and when the time is right. He knows exactly the kind of tests we need to be ready.

I see that first hand now, and as the days go by, I'm understanding why God prepared me in the way He did. I find myself having to put into practise the things I've learnt over the years.

I'll share a silly, but true story. One evening, before we were married, my honey and I went to this function. We had just eaten, and I opened my dinner mint. The wrapper read, "It's different this time." So, I showed EF it, and we were having our cute moment. So, we decided to open his and guess what his said, "It's different this time." We checked out the others on the table because we were like, "Nah, maybe they all say the same thing." It was only ours though.

God can be cute and use anything to send a message.

The thing about my husband is that he wanted to be married, and he came to a point in his life when he was ready for it. Consequently, he had started doing the things he needed to do to become 'husband material' way before we were actually together. I believe that when a man is ready for marriage, there's no guessing. A woman won't ever have to wonder where she stands with him or what he wants. He will make his intentions clear.

Thus far, marriage this time around has truly been very different from my first, and I'm so grateful for all that I went through in the wait.

DREGS

As we go through the experiences of life, we sometimes accumulate dregs…stuff that settles way below the surface because we could not cope with it at the time or life necessitated us to keep going.

When God is ready to expand our capacity, He needs to purge us of the dregs. God can't fill us to capacity if space is being taken up by junk and waste matter.

Often, the way to bring these dregs to the surface to be dealt with is by shaking up our lives. If I imagine my life as a bottle, those dregs only get to be poured out if the bottle is turned upside down or shaken up. Everything in our lives will be shaken by God.

In these moments of discomfort and shaking, we sometimes find ourselves reacting in ways that we don't desire to, or in ways we thought we had changed, but God knows what's inside of us, and just what to do to get out the dregs.

Sometimes, things have to come up before they come out.

So, when things come up, it's an opportunity for change and freedom. God is well able to complete the work He started in us. The fact that we still have breath means that He's not finished with us yet, and we still have hope.

Tran-

Si-

Tion

MR. WRIGHT-

SO WRONG AND YET SO RIGHT

If you'd said to me at the beginning of last year that I'd be married to my current husband, I would have laughed. I wasn't looking for God there at all. He's probably the last person that I would have considered.

Despite checking most of the boxes in terms of the qualities I asked God for, there were three major non-negotiables that weren't met and a few ones that I hadn't on my list. Yes, I did have a list. Why not? *If I can make a list when I go grocery shopping, why wouldn't I have one for such an important aspect of my life?*

Here's my list:

WHAT I NEED FROM A MAN IN A RELATIONSHIP

- ☐ One who is totally sold out for and walks with God & knows that JESUS is the Way and is not ashamed to say so
- ☐ One who knows himself and is comfortable in his own skin
- ☐ One who knows his purpose and is walking in it
- ☐ One who shares his dreams, fears, emotions, life with me
- ☐ AMBITIOUS, but not GREEDY
- ☐ CONFIDENT not Arrogant, yet HUMBLE
- ☐ Shows GENUINE Attention & Interest- without Me having to ask/beg for it
- ☐ Someone who cares about ME as a person
- ☐ One who has RESPECT
- ☐ A FRIEND
- ☐ One who will not encourage me to compromise my values
- ☐ One who is interested in my dreams,

goals, ambitions and will lend support and encouragement to attaining such

- ☐ One who is not threatened by MY success
- ☐ One who has insight into who I really am and deals with me in Knowledge
- ☐ One to whose dream and purpose, I can contribute naturally
- ☐ Someone whom I complement and vice versa
- ☐ One with a sense of humour
- ☐ A Romantic, Passionate Man who aims to please
- ☐ One who loves with his ALL
- ☐ One SLOW to ANGER
- ☐ FAITHFUL, Dependable and Trustworthy
- ☐ Generous
- ☐ EMOTIONALLY MATURE, Empathetic
- ☐ One with whom I'm comfortable sharing ALL of myself, with whom my HEART is SAFE
- ☐ One who is TURNED ON by me- mentally and sexually
- ☐ One who is genuinely interested in CHILO and will play an active role in his life
- ☐ One who wants a daughter
- ☐ One who manages his finances well
- ☐ One with whom I share common interests and world view
- ☐ One who is not too proud to LISTEN and take advice from his WIFE and Treats her as an EQUAL PARTNER
- ☐ One who can apologise easily and take responsibility for his actions
- ☐ One who does not hide things or keep secrets from me
- ☐ Someone who I find physically attractive, not too hairy on the chest, but it can be waxed. Will compromise here

- ☐ Someone with whom I share a deep connection. Who gets me and my essence and I don't need to explain everything
- ☐ One who can finish my sentences
- ☐ Someone who loves me unconditionally
- ☐ Someone who is able to express himself well and will deal effectively with conflict in a healthy, mature manner. Seeks to resolve issues rather than bury them
- ☐ One who is willing to do the work marriage sometimes takes
- ☐ One who is the spiritual head of his home
- ☐ One who knows that my duty is not just to cook, clean wash, but can and will do these things for himself and his family if need be
- ☐ A man who loves to cook (This is icing)
- ☐ One who understands order and priority.

Need I say that a man with seven children spread across three different women certainly did not make my husband material list. Neither did recovering drug addict or Fluff Master. I wouldn't even have imagined it, far less actually having to live with such a reality.

Added to that equation was divorced not once, but twice (from the same person). As if all that wasn't enough, there was that other non-negotiable.

I never thought that I would knowingly marry a man who doesn't believe that Jesus is the way and not just a way? (Yet, this is a place I know very well because I was there once.) I would be unevenly yoked, and that could never be the Lord, right?

Then, there's the issue of celebrity and women…the many, many, women who were, was and wish they were to come. I wasn't about to deal with that.

Isn't he just the kind of person that God loves to use though? He's great at taking the foolish things to confuse those who have 'got it all together.' (I'm included in this category). 'Despite my list,' God still had His way, and I needed to be open to what He was doing. So much about Errol was right, and in my mind, so much was wrong. He's my Mister Wright, and as it turns out, I married the Best Man for me.

I've been told by people, both men and women when I'm introduced as Mrs. Fabien:

- "Look how just so you become a celebrity. You nailed it!"
- "Girl, you real good! I had to meet the woman who got Errol to marry her"
- "How do you manage with him? He's not easy"
- "I will pray for you"
- "You must be a very special person for Errol to marry you"
- "How did you meet HIM?"
- "Please accept my sympathy"

- "Oh, I thought you were one of his daughters"

- "When I saw the pics, I said, "Dat is a trophy"

- "What's it like being married to a famous person?"

- "You must laugh every day"

- "Are you sure you're married to him?"

- "Finally, someone to control Errol"

- "How many times has he been married before?"

- "Girl, you took that chance?"

The things people say…I wasn't put off by any of these though, it's amusing most of the time. I know that I'm married to the man of God's choosing, therefore I made up my mind for whatever came along with it. I understand that he has a past, just as I do, and that my past was never held against me. I got to live it down. I know that God has had so much mercy on me and that the person I am today is not the person I used to be. More than this, I know who I am and what God has called me to. ***I'm a living testimony of the mercy of God and His transformational love.***

Errol and I are from two completely different worlds, the most unlikely people to be together, yet we are so well suited.

We are so different, and in many ways, we are cut from the same cloth. Truth be told, being Mrs. Fabien comes with huge responsibility, and is not as glamorous as it may seem from the outside. That being said, I was born for this, but it came at a price.

Years of preparation and sacrifice went into what seemed to be a 'suddenly.'

I know that I'm not the most physically attractive woman he could have had. I'm not the best cook or homemaker. I'm certainly not the most intelligent or qualified one by our standards, but I'm the woman God chose, the one He prepared for this man and the one He prepared this man for.

It was important to know that we didn't put ourselves together, so, when things come up, we trust God because we are clueless and incapable at best. God backs up His plans. Left up to me, I might have run a long time ago, but God had said from the very beginning,

"There is no fear in love, but perfect love casts out all fear because fear involves torment. But he who fears has not been made perfect in love." I John 4:18

I know the man I married. I've never had any delusions about him. I accept his past and all that comes along with it, and I appreciate that it has served to bring him to the place where he is right now. I also accept his present, and I love him where he is today, knowing that I too am fallible and a 'work in progress.'

Let me say here that it's not always easy, but so worth it. It forces me to look at myself, it necessitates dying daily…like any marriage requires. Most of all, I've had to embrace the invaluable gifts of 'Shut up' and 'Silence.'

God really had to change my mindset about many things. Mostly, the way He loves us and the way I viewed love. He used Errol and our relationship to show me how He loves and to open up chambers of my heart I didn't know were closed. Everything about our lives and our relationship was '***Out the Box,***' and required us both to come out of many more boxes to get to this point.

Indeed, God's really been doing a 'New Thing.' There's really nothing that I could have done to become Mrs. Fabien, it was all God Powered. 'Ah mean,' can you imagine meeting your husband on Charlotte Street? LOL!

If becoming Mrs. Fabien was my pursuit, we surely would not be married now. In fact, it was quite the opposite. I didn't try to change him or get him to be anything or any different way with me. Least of all, I didn't try to 'control' him…that would have been tantamount to witchcraft. I was just Jilean, I stood by what I believed, and I surrendered this relationship to God every step of the way.

I didn't give up 'the fluff' as he calls it or try to get him to be with only me. Truth be told, he never tried to get it. I wasn't trying to have him for myself, although there was a point when I knew that he was mine.

He had begun severing extraneous connections on his own before we were officially 'together.' He says that he was ready to be married, and had already begun to make the necessary changes in his life. As he says, he had already packed one hundred and fifty years of living into his fifty-eight years of life. He shared that he wanted something different, he desired something real and lasting. I think it was really about timing and purpose.

God took us both through our own processes to prepare us for a lifetime of marriage, and I am so grateful now for this because it enabled us to forge a very solid foundation on which to build our relationship. In hindsight, I understand why God had us do things in the way we did.

I prayerfully sought the Lord about our relationship-over and over. Interestingly, I used to pray for Errol way before we started communicating regularly. I would hear messages about praying for my husband before I met him. I can say that God had me doing this before I ever had a thought that Errol would be my husband.

I've known that I'm called to influence globally, and I knew that I needed to have a spouse who understood that I belonged to the world...someone who would be secure in who he is and not be threatened by all that comes with it.

I have never wanted to be seen and would much prefer to stay in the background and do whatever I have to. However, I accept my visibility and embrace my regality as Esther (from the bible) did because of His plans for my life.

Never had I thought that I would be the one who needed to adjust to being with a 'celebrity' and a man who belongs to the people of the world and all that comes along with that. God has such a sense of humour...

He showed off with Errol. He's so extra, I asked for a man with a sense of humour, and God gave me a comedian. I've laughed more in the last couple years than I have in the previous ten before Errol was in my life. It's really different this time around, and I'm grateful for all the beauty my

Heavenly Father has given me in this marriage for the ashes of the first.

HIGH DEFINITION

It's not enough to know what we don't want, but we must define exactly what we do want. It's important to get specific about what we desire. It helps to write the vision and make it plain.

The things we focus on are what we move towards and bring to ourselves. The things we fear come upon us. Fear focuses on the things we don't want and faith focuses on the vision we have for ourselves.

When I was living my life by what I did not want, guess what I got? I accepted things and relationships into my life that I assessed as suitable because they didn't check the box of something I didn't want. However, in most cases, I got different varieties of things I didn't want because I had not defined what I actually did want.

So, what do you want?

When I worked in HR Consulting, we worked with a Job Description when interviewing candidates for positions with our client. The client would share with us qualifications, technical competencies and characteristics of the individual they required. Our first step in the process after developing the candidate profile is to screen the resumes on the basis of basic qualifications.

Then, we looked at whether someone had the ability to do the job but didn't have all the qualifications. We had a 'yes' pile, 'no' pile and a *'maybe'* pile. Some candidates were an outright 'no' because they didn't make the basic requirements.

So, why would we not have at least a basic 'Potential Spouse Specification?' The person we marry is a huge decision, as it directly impacts on our ability to fulfil the purpose that God had set for us to accomplish together. Being joined to another person impacts on every area of our lives, and affects us physically, emotionally and spiritually.

Having defined *what,* we desire in a spouse enables us to see at a glance if someone is qualified to get our attention as it relates to romance and consideration for a lifelong commitment. We are better able to ascertain fit.

Having a vision for our lives, streamlines our efforts, thereby causing us to be more efficient and productive. It allows us to eliminate non-productive activities and ventures. Years ago, I did a strategic plan for my life. That document got packed in a box somewhere with all my moving. Recently however, I stumbled upon it and was quite in awe to see that I was walking out many of those things today, even though I was not intentionally following what I had written.

There were things in that document that were further defined later on when I did Vision Boards, not remembering what I had written before. I'm not sure how it works, except to say that it's a spiritual principle and God says to write it down and make it plain. I believe that He's the one who places certain desires in our hearts to begin with, so He works with us to bring them to pass.

God spoke His word, but He also had it written, and the written word became flesh and still comes to life through us. We are created in His image and likeness, therefore, we have the potential to manifest as He does.

The word of God says in Habakkuk 2:2,

And the Lord answered me and said, Write the vision, and make it plain upon tablets, that he may run that reads it. For the vision is yet for an appointed time, but at the end it shall speak and will not lie. Though it tarries, wait for it because it will surely come...But the just shall live by his faith.

Thoughts become words, and words become things. Not only do our words have power, but so do the pictures we see in our minds. Some may call it our imagination. This is why Vision Boards are so powerful, especially if you're a creative person. I've found them to be much more fun and expressive to develop.

Perhaps our writing it down is more about creating awareness for us, so that we can get on board with God's programme. Through faith, we are able to manifest the desires that God has already placed in our hearts. As we surrender to Him, His desires become our desires.

"Delight yourself also in the Lord, and He shall give you the desires of your heart. Commit your way to the Lord, trust also in Him, and He shall bring it to pass." Psalms 37: 4-5

It would be remiss of me not to share that as this chapter was being written, Gayelle the Caribbean was in the process of its relaunch in Full HD, a vision, that was written down many years ago. In fact, Errol already had the 'standee' made. We are thankful for the manifestation of this vision and look forward with great anticipation to all the 'New' that comes along with it.

HONOUR THY FATHER & THY MOTHER

Christmas 2018, when Errol had just started coming by to 'spend time', it raised a couple of red flags for my parents. I was confronted about their concerns by New Year's Day, but there remained some misconceptions that needed to be dispelled.

I wasn't angry, as I could understand why they would feel what they felt with the information that they'd been presented. I'd just wished that things could have been discussed a bit more. It was quite an odd situation since, at that point, Errol and I were not officially 'courting.' Nevertheless, he stopped visiting me at my parents' home.

After praying on the situation, the Lord told me to write my parents a letter. So, I did just that. By this time, we were officially a couple and Mr. Fab had been wanting to come and state his intentions.

In my letter to my parents, I expressed my love for them and my gratitude for all they had done for me. I cleared up any misconceptions, and I stated that if Errol proposed that I was going to say yes, but that I would prefer to have their blessing.

Also, that he would not propose until he had spoken to them first to seek their blessing. We wanted to start on the right foot, and a father's blessing makes a difference.

On Ash Wednesday, after both parents had read the letter, my mom told me that everything would be okay. So, Mr. Fab wasted no time.

That weekend, Errol came to state his desire and intention to marry me and to ask my parents' blessing. Having been nurtured in the 'old school,' he not only spoke to them, but he hand-wrote them a letter. My parents, knowing what he was coming to do, had prepared to toast post meeting. Needless to say, they gave their blessing and here we are.

If this was God as we believed it was, things had to be done His way and in His time. He's a God of order, and He backs His word. It is so important to honour our parents and those who have care over us. Would we have proceeded without it? If we had done everything possible (including going to my siblings) to have it, yes.

God is faithful.

On a side note: I believe that parents often see things that we may not, and it's always wise to listen and prayerfully consider what they have to say. Theirs is usually the voice of wisdom.

TELL HIM YES

We decided that we were going to church one Sunday morning in February 2019. I had been crying out to God to answer me concerning Errol once and for all. Is it yes or no? I so love this man…At 7:11, I saw the time and I knew that God was saying, ask for a sign. Isaiah 7:11

During song worship, the Lord and I were having a discourse in my head. He read my heart and asked me a question.

The conversation went like this:

Suppose, you were in the public and he said something that you thought misrepresented Me, what would you do?

I would support him Lord. We'd probably talk about it when we got home, but I would not oppose him in public or be embarrassed.

Would you give up your life for him?

Yes Lord, I would. He has done so for me in so many ways.

Would you die for him?

Yes Lord, I would.

Good, because I died for you when you were still a sinner because I loved you- right where you were. I never asked you to change this or that. I received you as you were. I was never ashamed of you.

His answer went straight to my heart. A peace flooded my being, and I knew in that moment His answer. (I'd been wanting to get this answer since that moment when our gazes locked, that day he first dropped into my office unexpectedly.) In that moment, The Lord said to me, *"Turn to him and tell him YES."*

So, I turned to Errol and I said, "Yes."

He said to me, "Wait, what is the question?"

"The answer is yes," I said. "Can I have that in writing," he said. I took out a pen, and I wrote the word, "YES" in his hand. I cannot describe the smile on his face and the joy I saw my answer bring to him.

When service was over, we went in one car up the highway to a meeting. Errol shared that he was having a conversation with God about wanting to know once and for all what the deal was with me. "J, you know that I don't really ask for signs and all that right. But this morning, on my way down, I said to Him, the word I wanted to hear in church is YES. I wanted an answer because I had had enough." I was a bit bewildered at these words. What if I had not obeyed?

As he drove, he was speeding ahead with his plans with respect to our marriage and life together, for he knew very early in our relationship that he wanted to be married to me. For me, I knew that as long as I got a 'Yes' from God to be with whoever, that that person would be my husband.

This is why it was so important for me to be sure. I did not have time to waste, and I don't believe in dating to see where things go. It got a bit too real for me hearing these plans so fast, and I got scared and started back-peddling…" Maybe, I should wait a while, pray and fast to make sure."

To him, it probably felt as though I had taken him up to a mountain top and dropped him to the earth all in the same day. This is how I describe what he said. It hurt me to even think that I'd hurt him, but failure at another marriage was not an option for me and after waiting ten years, I wasn't about to make a wrong choice.

I had to be sure that it was God and not my emotions leading me. For, I loved him so much. My friend, Shé says that I was '*bazodee*' over him. I agonised over hurting him and hearing correctly, and I talked to God about my confusion to which He replied "Be still."

The next morning, the Lord asked me, "*Do you realise what happened Jilean? You know Errol never asks me for anything, even after numerous people telling Him to ask Me for what he wants. Do you realise that yesterday morning, he asked me for you?*"

That peace flooded my heart again, and I knew I had to call him and tell him that my 'Yes' still stands.

So, I called him just as he finished signing 'the documents'...something he'd been waiting three years for. My 'Yes' on his walk from signing really moved his heart...and the plans were on the way. It is weird how we knew we wanted to be married, and I said "Yes" before being proposed to or actually being engaged. My 'Yes' was really saying, "I'm now released to be with you," which for me, meant that we were ultimately moving towards marriage. (The official proposal would not come until March 26, 2019. He says he could not propose to me without first purchasing a ring.)

As God would have it, Valentine's Day was the week before. He was not in the country, but had put everything in place for my week of roses before my 'Yes.' I had a different coloured rose delivered to my office every day of that week with a piece of a sentence.

Monday-White "So, I just wanted..."

Tuesday-Yellow "...To remind you..."

Wednesday-Lilac "...About how much..."

Thursday-Orange "...I love you!"

Friday-Red "Okay."

It was beautiful, and I felt like the only woman on earth-and still do. We were at one of those markets on the weekend before doing promotion for what is now, our brand, "God Powered Revolution." He got me the vase at the market on Saturday. It was the only one, but exactly what he had in mind. He flew out on Sunday, but left instructions to take the vase to the office on Monday, wash it out and fill it to one third with water - (this man of mine is very specific), as "Some things will begin to grow from it."

It was the most romantic thing anyone has ever done for me. Most people have a Valentine's Day, I had a week, but really, I feel as though, I have a lifetime. I never imagined what being treated 'like a Queen' would be like. Honestly, sometimes, it actually takes some getting used to and a lot of letting go of being 'self-sufficient.'

I had gotten so used to being single and having to see about everything myself, that it takes the grace of God to step back and allow myself to be husbanded. It's surreal at times, but I'm giving myself permission to just live and enjoy it.

THERE'S A TIME...

God's timing is perfect. We could miss the right alignment of many blessings when we move out of timing.

I got instructions to close my office in south in early February. The lease was actually up at the end of January, and we were owing for a month. So, the timing was great, the landlord could keep the month we had inside.

Little did I know that God was planning to send my confirmation about my relationship and that I'd be getting married and moving. That move also impacted our son, who was choosing subjects to go into Form 4 and would have had to transfer schools. His transfer was not disruptive, and his new school would prove to be better aligned to his personality and bent.

Ecclesiastes 3:1 says, *"To everything, there is a season and a time for every purpose under the heaven."*

There is a right time for things to happen, and when we move in our own strength and timing, we rob ourselves of ease and abundance and settle for less than God has for us.

His desire is always to far exceed our imagination or expectations. He always does more than we could think or ask.

God's denial isn't always 'NO.' Time can be our greatest ally. It allows for deeper intimacy, it allows for exposure and revelation.

There is favour in moving in the timing of God. There are people and resources that are moved into place for the 'right time.' Sometimes, we think that we need money to have certain things happen in our lives or to accomplish the vision that God has given, but all we really need is God's favour.

He is not limited by our sight, resources or our agenda. What usually takes a year to happen by human effort and striving, God can cause to happen in a day if He wanted it to. So, we don't need to be anxious or worried as long as we stay close to Him.

God provides for the vision He has given. Sometimes, the lack of that provision is a clue as to His timing for it, and an indication not to pursue it at that time. Perhaps, He has provided provision in a way, we can't yet see.

The following words have comforted and encouraged me at times when I was becoming frustrated with the wait.

> *Be anxious for nothing, but in everything by prayer and supplication, with thanksgiving, let your requests be made known to God: and the peace of God which surpasses all understanding will guard your hearts and minds through Christ Jesus. Philippians 4:6-7*

> *Seek ye first the kingdom of God and His righteousness, and all these things [food, clothing, things you have need of] shall be added to you. Therefore, do not worry about tomorrow, for tomorrow will worry about its own things. Matthew 6:33-34*

> *And let us not grow weary while doing good, for in due season, we shall reap if we do not lose heart. Galatians 6:9*

But without faith it is impossible to please Him, for he who comes to God must believe that He is and that He is a rewarder of those who diligently seek Him." Hebrews 11:6

Psalm 37 is too loaded to pull out verses.

If God has given you a promise, He will keep His word, but He will do it, His way and in His time. Keep the faith.

THE SIGNS

There were so many signs, although I chose to ignore many of them. I was so afraid to be carried away by my emotions. The more signs I got, the more I wanted.

I was introduced to Errol many years before when I had worked at a Management Consulting firm through a mutual friend of ours. He didn't remember this meeting; he was probably too captivated by my friend at the time. I was in my twenties then.

In December 2015, about twenty years later, I was invited by a friend to attend the café launch of a 'Relief Organisation' on Charlotte Street, Port of Spain. I explained that I didn't really want to go because I'd had a long week on the road, and felt like I just wanted to rest that Sunday evening. She shared that she really wanted me to come and that I could bring some T-shirts to market the brand.

Every mention of this event resulted in my body erupting in goosebumps. I've come to learn that this is one way in which the Holy Spirit bears witness with me. It was clear to me that He wanted me to attend this event for whatever reason.

I arrived at the event about fifteen minutes late. Not being familiar with the layout and run of the programme, I parked and went upstairs to scope out the scene, leaving the t-shirts in the car. I was assured it was okay to bring them, so I went back to the car for them. On getting to the doorway, I saw Errol standing there chatting with someone.

I greeted him, Good evening Mr. Fabien," he asked me how I was doing, I said, "Fine" to which he responded, "Yes you are." I laughed that comment off and continued up the stairs, as I had never stopped moving throughout this exchange.

I wasn't seated right away as I was dealing with t-shirt related matters. Next thing I know, Mr. Fab is upstairs and seated. When I was seated, it was on the same table as he was, directly opposite to him. That appeared to be the last seat in the house too. I remember thinking, "Why they seating me by him. Is there nowhere else?"

You'd think I would shut up right? Jilean started talking to the man. I was explaining how we had met through our mutual friend years ago. Then, it felt like we had shifted into an interview. We talked about Coaching and Women Out the Box.

He asked me about whether I had ever considered doing a show for the work I do with women to which I answered, "Yes, it's one of those things on my vision board actually. I'm not surprised that the conversation is happening, I'm just surprised at how quickly it is happening." He spoke about Gayelle, The Caribbean (his television station) and its reach throughout the Caribbean and the potential to earn more through visibility of my business. I was sitting there thinking, "God, you not easy..."

You see, a few weeks prior, I had received a prophetic word at church about how God was going to give me a platform to influence a lot of people and how He was calling me from the back to the front and that my voice would be heard.

Much earlier that year, a friend of mine shared a dream with me about our work with television. She didn't share at that time that Errol was one of the people in the dream. That would happen about a year later.

Mr. Fab left that evening with my business cards. I was prompted to follow up with him a couple days later. I messaged, but did not get a response at that time.

In August 2016, I moved back to my parents' home in south. My son had gotten through Secondary Entrance Assessment, and my lease was also up at my north apartment. What timing?

It would have been a day that year that I was driving down Wrightson Road saying to the Lord in my mind that if this Gayelle talk show thing was really His will that Errol would be under attack, and I should be praying for him more.

Within seconds of having the thought, it came over the news that he had been in a car accident in St. Lucia. I couldn't believe my ears, but I suppose God answered me in the affirmative.

It would be more than a year after our meeting at the 'Relief Organisation' and my FB message that I'm in a prayer and fast about business strategies (July 2017), and the Lord told me to try contacting him again. I messaged, and this time he responded. It was so strange for me to be messaging him here and there, hoping that he'd bring up the show. He never brought it up...So, I would just drop a word of encouragement and good vibes for the day.

One evening at church, a friend in whom I had confided about all these goings on, said to me, "Jilean, it's time for you to talk to Errol." I explained that I had already been in contact, to which she replied, "No, it's time for you to be direct." This was around November 2017.

I did a 3-day prayer and fast for clarity. I had a hesitation in contacting him because I was unsure what I was going to say about the show and how I was going to present it. I didn't want to seem like 'I wasn't ready yet.' On the second day, the Lord told me to make contact because I didn't have to have it all worked out. Just schedule the meeting and He will direct it.

So, I messaged Errol asking whether he had been serious about the show and whether he had any specific direction for it. He said that he was serious and that he didn't have a specific direction and asked whether I did. I indicated that I had a few ideas but that it would be great to meet to discuss them further. He agreed and said that he would check his schedule and get back to me by Thursday of that week, and that I should call if I didn't hear from him because he gets busy.

On Thursday, we scheduled for the following Monday. We did the first pilot on December 22nd and met again for another shoot on Christmas Eve. Early in the New Year, Mr. Fab shows up unexpectedly at my office in south with another comedic friend. I don't know how the conversation wound up on people with the four of us and became very heated. There was a moment here where our eyes met and we held that gaze for a few seconds. Oh boy…

We had been communicating a bit more since the shoot as we were editing the opening sequence for the show, and it would be almost a year again before we got back to 'show business,' but he featured prominently in my life.

During the time in between, I would say, we were becoming great friends fully aware of the chemistry between us, but very respectful and platonic. You see, I believed that

God was telling me 'No' about being with him because his first and second wives were still alive (same person). As if one non-negotiable wasn't enough, he wasn't sold out for Jesus either.

To make matters worse, Mr. Fab told me that he wasn't even sure whether he was actually divorced because he never saw the final documents, but had signed all the necessary papers. He said that it was very awkward to ask for them. Sister Jilean was determined that nobody was going to say that she is a home wrecker, least of all, the children, as up until that time, they were never told of their parents' second divorce.

The signs were all there though. Lord knows that I asked for many. I got most of these before my 'Yes' and some thereafter:

- The many prophetic words about the timing of our meeting. Although, I didn't see it coming or recognise him as my husband when it happened

- The altar-call for singles asking us whether we were willing to let go of the 'type' or preconceived notions about how our husbands will come

- They say that a husband recognises his wife. Errol says, he knew very early on that he'd be married to me, and he told me, "I am going to marry you" when it seemed to me that nothing could be further from the truth. He says that God told him that he was to stay by my side, serve and protect me

- Prophetic words about having a platform to reach many people. I think cable television qualifies

- The qualities I asked for and this knowing in the recesses of my being that I could not escape despite the question marks. This too was the unfolding of a prophetic word that even though I'd need to make sure, there'd be a 'knowing'

- The pastor friend calling me from the USA to confirm that an 'us' was in the will of God. I had asked God for someone outside of Trinidad and Tobago to call and confirm that this relationship was leading to marriage. This particular friend is the last person I expected to say what she said. So much so, I never gave her any details about us (except for business) or the fact that I loved him prior to this phone call. She asked me some direct questions. It's like she was on a mission. Even when she spoke prophetically into our marriage, she too acknowledged that she was speaking under instruction because she would not have thought to tell me those things based on how she normally would have thought about the both of us being together. I knew it was God because unbeknown to her at that time, He had answered my specific prayer for that sign

- Long before he was in my life, another friend

had said that my husband-to-be would come home and ask my father's blessing to marry me. Not only did Errol do this, but he also wrote them a letter (with my never having shared what was said or asking for it)

- Alignment of purpose and the synergies between us

- A dream I had about the person I would marry outlining the sequence of events

- There was an encounter that happened while sitting in the front porch of his home. Although the incident happened in the spirit realm, we both felt it. More specifically, I physically felt when the thing happened to him. I had never experienced anything like that before

- More often than not, we meet each other dressed in the same colors, or complementing each other, totally unplanned. One such time was our meeting at the Socadrome. My friend said to me the night before not to fuss about what I was going to wear because God already planned a surprise for me. On the day, I wore a top with a cami below, but felt this leading to walk with my red God Powered *(GP)* t-shirt. When I arrived at the venue, he was wearing his red GP Tee, so I just put mine on in the car. It was all God Powered and God was confirming it

- The matching wrappers saying, 'It's different this time

- The favour for the wedding. My chef friend being in Antigua when it's not where he was 'supposed to be.' With God, there are no coincidences. I would often say to him that I wanted him to cater my wedding. I never knew that I was going to have a destination wedding in Antigua and that he was going to be based at a hotel there at the precise time that we would be planning to get married

- The precise timing of the close of my office in south and when God told me to say "Yes." When I closed the office, I didn't know yet that days ahead, I would get my green light. Also, the fact that my son was choosing subjects for form 4 and the impending move. The timing was perfect

- Prophetic words about my moving back to north

- My parents' blessing

- The initial date set for the wedding coincided with a guiding scripture, "*Love does not behave itself unseemly, seeks not itself, is not easily provoked, thinks no evil.*" Errol was looking at his schedule and asked about what the number 5:13 (May 13th) was in scripture. It's I Corinthians 13:5. Even though, we had to change our actual day to the 15th because of legal requirements, the initial suggestion was a sign that God was in the details.

Between the time when God told me 'No' and then told me to tell him 'Yes,' so much processing was done by Him with us both. Errol had gone on the 'Walk to Freedom' and had attended two Grief to Grace Retreats. He shared how the sessions helped him to come to the place of having those healing and divorce conversations with God, himself and those he cared about and how he had gone through a process of severing soul ties from previous relationships and encounters.

I had come to a different place of freedom in Christ and from the thoughts and opinions of others, especially in the church. I shifted from fellowshipping with the part of the church body I was assigned to for the season I was now exiting, to be the church in the spheres that I'm called to. He had been preparing me for marketplace ministry all along. I was learning how to love without fear. I was being humbled and positioned to be a wife who was able to be husbanded after being unattached for so long. Many old religious and inaccurate mindsets were purged. ***(A religious mindset can keep us more bound than any strategy the enemy can concoct. It's like an auto-immune disease.)***

Errol says that he knew even from our 'first' meeting on Charlotte Street that it was no ordinary meeting. There's something he saw in me, but he felt that he wasn't in a place yet where he was ready for me. This is why he'd never responded when I had messaged the first time after our meeting, but he trusted that we would reconnect at the right time, God willing.

I had heard messages about how God presents a wife to her husband, and he knows that she is bone of his bone and flesh of his flesh. I kept seeing 2:22 and Genesis 2:22 says that God made woman from the rib which was taken from man and brought her unto him (paraphrased). I have to say that I believe this is what happened with us. He says now that God told him very early on that I was his and that he was to serve me and protect me. He also said to me that he was going to marry me very early on…as though I had nothing to do with it.

It took me much longer to get to the place where I 'knew beyond a shadow of doubt,' especially because of my history with God and being 'bound till death' to my first husband. (Errol was not always a happy camper because I tried to sever our relationship twice and there were a few times when I went 'off the grid.' He had the patience of Job with me…and still does. Birthday 2018, I spent in Barbados. I wanted so much to spend it with him, and he was willing to come, but God said "Wait." At least, He didn't say, "No," right?)

He did say that He was doing a 'new thing' though, and if I was to embrace the new, I had to be willing to release the old. I see how anchoring myself in that word (I Cor.7:11) had kept me safe and preserved me up until the time that I'd met Errol. Also, it allowed me to remain pliable in God's hands and to experience a deeper dimension of His love. I came to understand His heart and His motivation.

There is one more non-negotiable that I haven't mentioned…This one should have put the nail in Errol's coffin for me. Yet, despite, how he felt, he lay down his life in this area because he desired to be married to me.

So, when God asked me if I would lay down my life for him, my answer could only have been 'Yes.'

I trusted him to honour his word to me because he had proven himself to be an honourable man up until that point. There were three deliverables I was promised, and I only got them the week prior to our wedding. I suppose in his own way, it was a test of my love for him. Would I have married him still had I not gotten them? Yes, because I love him, but more so because I trust God, and I know that His hand was on this relationship from jump. I'd been given glimpses into his future and ours. My faith is in knowing that our union was His idea, and He is committed to fulfilling His word. God had already told me to say, 'Yes' and that's all I needed to know.

When the request for two of these deliverables was made, it was about me doing due diligence, but by the time, I received them, my position on them was different because of the trust I had in him and that God was joining us together. So, He would not give me a stone for bread. Only one of the three deliverables was necessary for us to get married. It was a legal requirement, otherwise, I would not have bothered.

God speaks to me in many ways, and I'm sure He'll find many more. He's not limited to my finite thinking.

HOW GOD SPEAKS

The Lord asked me specifically to put in this chapter at this moment. So, if you're wondering how it came in, now you know. Take it up with Him. There are some ways that God speaks that are common to everyone, and then there are some that are very personal and individual. You will learn which are specific to you the more you develop your relationship with Him.

Primarily, He speaks through His written word, and would not contradict it, but sometimes, His spoken word (whether to our hearts or through His messengers) may give specifics not found in the word, but we know it's Him through our intimate relationship. We know His heart, His character and His essence.

Yes, He does speak through people, whether through a sermon or a friend or a prophetic word from a total stranger, but we must try the spirit, through the filter of His word, and whether His peace accompanies it. Often, when someone says something to me, God has already spoken through the word or directly to my heart, so I tend to know whether that person's word is from Him or not.

God has used e-mails to speak to me before. He's spoken through songs, movies, jokes, scents, sounds, sights, words, numbers, questions, other people's dreams, physical feelings in my body, clouds in the sky.

I sometimes ask for confirmation or a sign. I get specific about the sign, but not always. God knows how to get a message to us. Some people disagree with this, but it works for me. Why wouldn't God confirm something if He wants me to do it? He did it with Gideon in the Bible.

I have had an instance though when He was being very silent, but it was because He had already spoken on the matter, and He knew that I knew He had. So, He said, "Jilean, I already answered you about that, and you know what you have to do."

Next, He speaks to me through dreams, visions, pictures in my head, and thoughts that come to my mind. I can also have very lucid dreams where I'm able to interact in them and make choices. Not all dreams, visions, thoughts or imaginations are from Him though. We need to ask for clarification, wisdom and discernment.

I also have the gift of interpretation which He's still developing in me, but He's proven that I do flow in that. Even if I didn't know it, people tend to just share their dreams with me. This is a gift I have because I asked for it. It made sense to me that I should have this gift given that I am a dreamer.

He also speaks through His peace. When I don't have peace about something, it is an indication to pay closer attention. It may mean "Don't proceed," but it may also mean that I'm supposed to do that thing that I keep running away from. It could also mean, "Stop fighting me and surrender Jilean."

He speaks to me when I'm in conversations, and I get goosebumps as a witness that He's in it.

Oh, and then there are the prophetic numbers. I thought that I was being strange, but it was undeniable. Now, I know it happens to many other people too. I'd see numbers everywhere, repeated throughout the day. They just jump out at me. It started with just number plates, 777. I can sometimes in a half hour see about 5. The car could be parked in a garage and I would see it.

Now, I see numbers on billboards, on the clock, phone, laptop, on people's clothes, a book, they can be anywhere. The numbers I see now are more sophisticated and also, they often correspond to scripture. I could be having a phone chat with someone and see a time stamp and know in the moment what the word is for that person.

God can speak through an audible voice. He has done so with me a few times before, but it's very rare. He is not limited in His ability to communicate. Once we take Him *'out the box'* and remain open to Him, we'll get the messages. I know He's always speaking, but I'm not always in the place to hear Him, or the static of my own thoughts or other people's can affect my ability to hear. It sometimes takes practise to be still and know…

ASCENSION

I commissioned Prophetic Artist, Lana Ramasray to do a painting guided by a few specific verses of scripture...Words the Lord had given to me. She was not told what to paint. This was the rendering.

This painting has a special place in my heart because it was as though God sent me something tangible from His heart to mine. You see, the year before I got this, a friend was praying for me and she described this very painting, except she said that as I ascended the steps, there was a man waiting there for me.

Lana had no way of knowing this...

I hadn't known when she would have delivered it, but the night before she presented me with it, I was watching the movie "One Night with the King," the story of Esther. I was bewildered when I saw what she had painted.

The painting reminded me of Esther ascending the steps to approach the king, and confirmed a call on my life. Such is the nature of the prophetic. This is why I specifically didn't tell her what to paint because I wanted it to be directed by Him and not me. It's more impactful that way.

Errol commented on seeing this painting and the 'Love' one that there seemed to be a theme of 'Ascension' in my life.

BIBLICAL THINGS OUT THE BOX

Speaking of taking Him *'out the box,'* there are a few things in the Bible that have come to light for me that I've overlooked in the past when discussing these characters and verses.

ESTHER

Esther was placed in the palace by God to help bring deliverance to His people. The King, Ahasuerus was not a king of Israel, but he loved and favoured Esther so. In effect, Esther was 'unevenly yoked with an unbeliever,' yet it was the will of God for a purpose much greater than herself.

Furthermore, Esther was married to a divorcee. Yes, she became Queen because it was God's will, but also because the king had divorced Vashti. Favour, just ain't fair…

Esther was called upon to go against the law of the land and approach the king unannounced, knowing that she could perish as a result, but choosing to honour God. Go against the law? We see Daniel doing this as well in his determination to remain faithful to God.

So, to all who are called to be Esthers, you may want to adjust your lenses or expectations a bit. Think about what it may entail…the cost. Can you love a man who does not fit what you had in your mind or what you've been taught all your life you should not look for? How important are external appearances to you or the opinions of others? How willing are you to go against the grain, the status quo, to be obedient to God? Suppose it means that people think you're rebellious or that you've backslidden? Suppose it means that you no longer have the support of the Who's Who? Suppose it means that your family members won't speak to or live with you? Are there limits to what you would do if you knew that something was God's will for your life?

HOSEA

Hosea had specific instructions from God to take Gomer, a prostitute as his wife. As if that wasn't enough, he had to take her back every time she stepped out on him…going as far as to buy her back in the market.

Can you imagine how painful that all must have been? It was hard enough being married to a prostitute, but can you imagine the people on the outside talking about his wife, about him and how much of a *'chupidee'* (see glossary) he is? "He didn't need flambeau to see in the night what was so clear in de day."

I don't know about you, but if I knew that someone was going to marry a prostitute, I would question whether it was God's will, but here we have an instance where it was a directive from God. His ways don't always make sense.

God used Hosea to act out His unconditional love before the people. He was trying to show them and us that every time we go astray and commit spiritual adultery, He takes us back. He went as far as to send Jesus to pay a price with His life to buy us back.

This story came to bear in my life when I was told that I was bound to my ex till death and that I could only be with him for as long as he remained alive. That was the toughest request of God in my life up until that time. He said to me that I was to mirror unconditional love to him, and that he would be a new creature in Christ. So, post-divorce while he was playing the field, I was not permitted to have any romantic relationships, not even online (there's a story here).

JONAH

We know how the story goes. Jonah disobeyed God and went on a ship to Tarshish when he should have been on a ship to Nineveh. There are two things I want to highlight about the story of Jonah.

Even though Jonah went his own way, he belonged to God, and therefore had to do what God required of him in the first place. God has a way of orchestrating things for us to walk in His will.

Secondly, there's something significant that happened on that ship to Tarshish. Due to the violent weather that arose as a result of Jonah's presence on the ship, the mariners cried out to the Lord for their lives. Immediately, after throwing Jonah overboard as he had instructed them to do, the sea ceased raging immediately. The scripture says, *"Then the men feared the Lord exceedingly, and offered a sacrifice unto the Lord and made vows." Jonah 1:16*

We are told that Jonah was *"fleeing from the presence of the Lord." Jonah 1:10* It's interesting how he thought that this was possible at all. Obviously, he could not escape the presence of God or pull one over on Him. All things worked together for good, for in Jonah's attempt at escape, it caused everyone on board that ship to acknowledge, beseech and commit themselves to the Lord.

Likewise, I can relate crying out to God in the midst of my life storms. In fact, these storms have a way of driving me straight into the arms of our loving Father.

ABRAHAM

We see Abraham and Isaac going up the mountain to sacrifice Isaac, the son of promise. However, we think of Abraham being the one who was being tested, but we see no struggle or protest from Isaac about being bound and placed on the altar, especially after he's told that God was going to provide himself a lamb for the sacrifice. It seems as though Isaac was readily laying down his life. We seldom talk about what Isaac may have been going through. Could he not have run away or put up a fight? Could he have felt betrayed?

Furthermore, prior to this test, Abraham is told to leave the place he knows as home to go to an unknown place that God will show him. What would his family have been going through? They too were leaving their home because Abraham said God instructed him to.

When God asked me to place Errol on the altar, it hurt knowing that he had done nothing to deserve that and I loved him so. Perhaps, one day, he'll tell his side of the story. Errol, it seemed was my promise, the man I'd been waiting for all this time, and God was asking me to give him up.

Yet, in the midst of it, God showed me that we were both walking this journey. Genesis 22:8 says,

> *"And Abraham said, 'My son, God will provide himself a lamb for the burnt offering': so,* ***they*** *went* ***both*** *of them* ***together****."*

I held on to this word believing that God would work everything out and my Isaac would live… I mean, my Errol would be mine. A friend of mine also said to me prophetically a few weeks prior to God's request that I should just give God my all and do as He says, and that He would provide a 'ram in the thicket.' This was a direct reference to Abraham's test, and having God direct me to this scripture through seeing numbers, it served as a confirmation and comforted my heart.

Well, I did give up Errol, even though we weren't really 'together' officially. I think in our hearts, we both knew that we were bound to each other, but God…

He's so faithful. You know how the story ends, or should I say began on May 15, 2019 on the island of Antigua, when I officially became *Mrs. FABien.*

There is so much purpose connected to this union, some of which I'm yet to discover. I probably wouldn't be alive and in this place today if '*good ole'* Father Abraham had not been obedient in offering up Isaac.

It is because he hadn't withheld his son, that God was faithful not to withhold His. If Jesus never came and paid the price He did, so many lives would have suffered. Suppose, I didn't release Errol, how would things have been different, I wonder? We may never know all the things and people connected to our decisions. Whose life depends on your obedience?

God never asks us to give up something unless He intends to give us something better. He does so much more than we could ever think or ask. That's why I ask BIG.

THE WORKS

"But will you know O vain man that faith without works is dead? James 2:20

I often hear this quoted when people are trying to tell you that you need to get up and take action in the direction of what you desire. For example, if you want to buy a car, you have to go to the dealer and test drive it. Usually, the thing that one has to do is connected to the thing that is desired. This is not wrong per say, but journey with me for a moment.

May I submit to you that the 'works' are whatever God has asked us to do in a situation, and that the works may not seem to be connected to the desired outcome in any way. It may be a totally unrelated thing. In other words, what God asks us to do (by faith in Him) does not always seem logical or make sense in our understanding. How can we say we have faith in God and be afraid or hesitant to take action on His instruction? How can we say we have faith and neglect to do the works?

People often say that God says, "He helps those who help themselves," yet this is found nowhere in scripture.

The works aren't the religious things we do that we think are in service to him either. He makes that clear in the following verses.

Not everyone who says to me, 'Lord, Lord' shall enter the kingdom of heaven, but he who does the will of My Father in heaven. Many will say to Me in that day, 'Lord, Lord, have we not prophesied in Your name, cast out demons in Your name, and done many wonders in Your name?' and then, I will declare to them, 'I never knew you; depart from Me, you who practice lawlessness!' Matthew 7:21-23

HOW SHALL MEN SEE GOD?

I've heard it over and over, "Without holiness, no man shall see God." It's usually used to mean that if we aren't holy, then we won't see God.

Here is the verse as it appears,

"Pursue peace with all people, and holiness, without which no one will see the Lord." Hebrews 12:14

I am no Bible scholar, but one day, I heard the Lord say to me, *"Jilean, without your holiness, people won't see me."* People are waiting to see and experience God through us.

THE PRIVATE WEDDING

Private does not mean secret. It just means that we didn't have guests except God and our two witnesses (both of whom are Antiguan). It means we didn't want a media circus. It was not elopement because there were those who knew about what we were going to do...only those who needed to know.

Having both been married before, we just wanted something personal and special to us and let's not forget economical. Did we pay a price for choosing to have a private wedding? Certainly, and we are still paying in ways that can't be discussed now, but we had the perfect wedding day. We got to spend it the way we wanted to. There were going to be more than enough things in our lives happening before the world in our future together.

There were those who were terribly hurt, extremely offended, immensely inspired, profusely elated, insanely jealous, quite surprised, overly concerned, highly intrigued, hugely curious and eternally supportive. None of the reactions to this union were mild...

"What was the rush?"

"She must be pregnant."

"What's her motive?"

"Where she come from?"

"We'll see how long this lasts"

"Like she back-slide..."

Why couldn't it be that we simply *love each other*? God joins people together for PURPOSE. It's not just about love, but love is lovely, and it's beautiful when we can have both. Had we considered everyone's feelings, we would have moved out of the will and timing of God. The wedding had to happen when it did or it probably wouldn't have happened at all, and all the things that were put into motion as a result would have been affected as well. Many people's lives would have been very different. Some of them, in their minds might have been much happier too, but God…

Perhaps, if we had weighed the cost, we might have tried to do things differently or not. ***But*** when Jesus says 'Yes,' nobody can say otherwise.

Oh Yes, there is one more factor in this equation (although, it was not a driving force) …that of 'The Fluff.' Having been a 'born again virgin' for ten years, and having been certain of God's will, there was no reason to prolong our wait time for marriage if we were to honour God in our waiting to be intimate sexually. Our intimacy and urge to merge had been growing rapidly as the days went by. What am I saying? I'm saying that there was 'no fluff' until our wedding night.

And, what of the Facebook posts? Well, I think we were just as entitled as anyone else to share our happy moment, especially since we hadn't been able to share before about our relationship and leading up to the wedding.

(It was hard enough just trying to spend an evening out without people coming up to EF for a picture or something. Can you imagine word getting out about a marriage in Trinbago?)

We so wanted to be together and wanted people to know, but Jilean wanted to be sure it was God's will…We didn't know until we did, so there was no way we could have let others know that we were together before February 2019.

After waiting ten years to be in a relationship, I think I deserve to be happy and to shout it from the rooftops about this amazing man God has blessed me with. He was well worth the wait.

THE SPACE

I've come to recognise the importance of allowing people a space to be who they are at whatever stage in life that they're at. Maybe, it's my 'Coach' training to give people a space free of judgement, but it is undeniable, the unconditional love of God is transformative.

More importantly, people should know that they're OK and enough - right where they are for whatever is required of them at that point.

This is what we have with God. We always have a non-judgmental space to come boldly into His loving arms, regardless of where we are at or what we've done. When we can live down stuff, it allows us to have hope for a better tomorrow. He never condemns us. He who has been forgiven much, loves much.

We can only do what we can, and we can only give what we have. Even then, we need the grace of God to enable us.

I've also learnt that when we provide that space, and people begin to grow, we must be flexible enough to acknowledge their growth and be able to flow with them where they've come to. This means, a continuous 'letting go' of our own expectations of them or their past failings. We are constantly evolving into who we were created to be.

Recently, I had an experience where someone grew so much that it challenged my sense of where I was at, but it also motivated me to strive for better. I had to adjust because the person had shifted. Sometimes, we can discourage those we work with when we keep treating them like they still are where they used to be.

Sometimes, the thing we think God is doing is not the thing that He's actually doing, but it's important to remain open and hold a space for possibilities.

Sometimes, we can be way off, and often, He does so much more than we could have ever imagined.

Some months ago, I visited a home to do vision boards with a couple people. A vision board is a visual form of a strategic plan for your life. It can include pictures, quotes, craft and anything else that excites, motivates and empowers you to chase your dreams. The idea is that we begin to move in the direction of what we focus on or pay attention to.

An individual who 'happened to pass by' inquired what we were doing. He got so excited that he decided to do one too. I asked him a few questions to get him started. After, I had left, he was doing his board well into the evening.

The thing is, God had already started preparing him to do it, as he had asked himself some of the same questions while away at work and had written down his answers. Also, he was speaking to a friend he had met recently who had told him about how she had done one and how much it had helped her.

He had laughed it off at the time, but when he saw us, he figured that God was talking to him about *this thing* and decided to do his.

Months later, he has manifested some things he had on there and is even surpassing much of what is on there. He is flying our country's flag high internationally and traveling the world doing what he loves.

If no one had believed in this young man years ago, he may have been strung out on drugs or dead. Now, he's on fire and living a life many only dream about and he's excited about all the possibilities that await him.

A few things are noteworthy about this story:

- With God, all things are possible
- Believe in your dreams
- We can move beyond our past
- We are only limited by ourselves
- Write the vision and make it plain. Habakkuk 2:2-4. This is a spiritual principle that works. Words become things
- God pitches multiples. He can exceed our expectations. His reach is far beyond our focus
- A person in the background may be someone who God has a special blessing for. Ignore no one
- Today I'm not who or where I used to be. Let's not be too quick to give up on people. A little grace goes a long way.

TALKING 'BOUT EVERYTHING

Talking about everything is a nice ideal, but in reality, things don't play out that way. Sometimes, we don't share, not because we don't want to, or because we are hiding things, but wisdom dictates. **Silence can be our greatest ally and is often the wisest thing we can do.**

Even God doesn't share everything with us all at once because we may not be in a place to handle it or understand it. If He had shown me everything that was to come, I may not have made certain decisions because of the price I would be required to pay.

Sometimes, the WHOLE picture can be overwhelming, and it's best to live in His grace just for today.

"Don't worry about tomorrow for tomorrow will take thought for the things of itself. Sufficient unto the day is the evil thereof." Matthew 6:34

Sharing things 'out of time,' can result in unwanted and unnecessary drama.

MONEY MATTERS

I do tithe, but not in the same way as I used to. What that means is, I put the money aside, and I distribute it as God leads. I do not just give it to an organised 'church,' but I ask Him to direct my giving, and that is often much more than ten percent.

Sometimes, it's the full amount to one person, and sometimes it is split up, and there are times when it is given in a church. There have been too many times to mention when the amount that I give to people is so precise in relation to their needs, that it confirmed for me that it was His doing.

I've had much and I've had little, but in all, I've never stopped tithing, and God has been faithful. The stretching of what remains happens in different ways. I've often heard people say that they can't afford to tithe given their commitments. It is my position that I can't afford not to because of its benefits. In the first place, all that I have should be available for use as He instructs, for it is by His grace that it was obtained. God blessed me by giving me all that He has, therefore what is ten percent to do as He directs?

Bring all the tithes into the storehouse, that there may be food in My house, and try Me now in this, says the Lord of Hosts,' if I will not open for you the windows of heaven and pour out for you such blessing there will not be room enough to receive it.
And I will rebuke the devourer for your sakes, so that he will not destroy the fruit of your ground, nor shall the vine fail to bear fruit for you in the field,' says the Lord of Hosts; and all nations will call you blessed...Malachi 3:10-12

It is a source of contention whether tithing is for today, if it's a new-testament or old-testament thing, whether it was adopted by the churches to bring money into the church, and whether the church really is the storehouse. All of that is irrelevant to me because it's between God and me. I've put God to the test, and He has proven Himself faithful. **My obedience to God is not contingent on what anyone else is doing or not doing. I accept full responsibility for my walk.**

My understanding of tithing is in the spirit of the law and not the letter of the law. The reason for tithing as stated in Malachi was that there would be 'meat/food in His house' or provision for His people. If we look at the book of Acts, we see where people sold their possessions and brought the proceeds and lay it at the feet of the apostles for distribution as there was need.

Now the multitude of those who believed were of one heart and one soul; neither did anyone say that any of the things he possessed was his own, but they had all things in common. And with great power the apostles gave witness to the resurrection of the Lord Jesus. And great grace was upon them all. Nor was there anyone among them who lacked; for all who were possessors of lands or houses sold them, and brought the proceeds of the things that were sold, and laid them at the apostle's feet; and they distributed to each as anyone had need. Acts 4:32-35

In both cases, it was a way for God's people to distribute to God's people, so that everyone's needs would be met. That's practical and loving.

Secondly, tithing for me is about trusting God, especially in an area so close to my heart, for 'money answers all things.'

Tithing is about faith and relationship. Tithing to me, is like God asking,

- "Do you trust me to provide for you beyond what you see?"

- "Will you trust me to prove to you that I am who I say I am?"

- "Do you have faith in Me? Then, put your money where your mouth is."

I believe it is important for us to be in a place where our identity is firmly rooted in Christ, and we are not led by our emotions before God bestows His mega riches on us, or we'll be easily swayed and won't distribute as He desires.

I'll share an experience I had. A friend of mine was close to losing her apartment and asked me for a loan. I had this money, but I told her that I needed to ask Him first. In my emotions, I would have loaned the money without blinking, but I realised later that it was not what He desired. There was a greater work He wanted to do.

When I sought the Lord, tithing kept coming up. So, when we spoke again, I asked her whether she had started tithing the last time He had me speak to her about it. She said that she had not, and I replied that I believe that this is what He is raising again. If I had cared more about being seen as 'nice' or about preserving the friendship or about her losing the apartment over what He desired, I would have loaned the money.

That friend did not respond in anger at the time…at least not to my face, and later thanked me for the stance that I took, as she was able to see the hand of God move in her situation. Her faith was increased and she now has relational knowledge of the faithfulness of God, and proof that His principles work.

SOME THINGS I'VE LEARNT ABOUT MONEY

- It's not more valuable than the favour of God
- It can't buy real love, but real love can yield infinite possibilities and priceless commodities
- It increases when you give it away to the right people and sources
- It can bring us happiness when we use it to create happiness for others
- Its multiplication factor depends on which 'kingdom' we choose to live in and the principles we apply
- When we release it, it comes back to us
- The abundance or scarcity of it can cause people to behave strangely
- If we aren't faithful in little, God won't trust us to give us much

- Utilising our gifts and walking in purpose attracts favour and provision

- Money is close to our hearts, God can use it or the lack of it to get our attention and break our hearts to receive more love

There are many money stories I could share, but maybe those are for another book or talk.

A Shift In Tone...

VENTING WITH HIM

Perhaps, those who live on the outside of the Church matrix, or who are unplugged from the religious system see things as they truly are.

I think in many cases, they aren't running from You, God, but they're fighting to be free. They want to be loved and to live and be accepted for who they are, but don't know that they are already accepted by You. I see myself in them. I know that I wasn't created to be caged, but to soar.

I know your love and truth when I experience it, and I think most people do too. After all, you created us to abide in Your Love. I didn't want to come into the church to be put under more bondage. I didn't want my peculiarity stifled in the name of submission to man-made doctrines. I don't think that I was always conscious of this though. I just knew when things rubbed me wrong, and I know your word.

What I see now is the problem as it was then:

> *"These people draw near to Me with their mouth, and honour Me with their lips, but their heart is far from Me, teaching as doctrines, the commandments of men."*
> *Matthew 15:8-9*

Too often, leaders in 'The Religious System' want people to adhere to things they don't even do. The pyramid of the world system is the same in the religious system, but anyone who is great, should first be a servant.

Lord, You summed it up here:

The scribes and Pharisees sit in Moses' seat. Therefore, whatever, they tell you to observe, that observe and do, but do not do according to their works; for they say, and do not do. For they bind heavy burdens, hard to bear, and lay them on men's shoulders; but they themselves will not move them with one of their fingers.

But all their works they do to be seen by men. They make their phylacteries broad and enlarge the borders of their garments. They love the best places at feasts, the best seats in the synagogues, greetings in the marketplaces, and to be called by men, "Rabbi, Rabbi."

But you, do not be called 'Rabbi;' for One is your Teacher, the Christ, and you are all brethren. Do not call anyone on earth Your Father, for One is your Father, He who is in heaven. And do not be called teachers; for One is your teacher, the Christ. But He who is greatest among you shall be your servant. And whoever exalts himself will be humbled, and he who humbles himself shall be exalted.

But woe to you, scribes and Pharisees, hypocrites! For you shut up the kingdom of heaven against men; for you neither go in yourselves, nor do you allow those who are entering to go in. Matthew 23:2-13

Thank you for telling me in Galatians 5:1 to:

"Stand therefore in the liberty by which Christ has made us free, and do not be entangled again with a yoke of bondage."

We can be so un-relatable sometimes, and we speak a language too difficult to understand. It's almost as though we don't want people to understand. What's wrong with simple everyday English, or better yet, Trini? What's wrong with being a human being and using a bit of empathy?

You speak with such simplicity. The language of love for all to understand, connecting with us through relationship and heart.

"...to the weak, I became weak that I might win the weak. I have ***become all things to all men****, that I might by all means save some." I Corinthians 9:22*

Shouldn't we be able to relate to people where they are at and forge relationships, so that we can influence through God's love? I remember where I used to be and how certain things rubbed me.

Seems like the more we know, the less we see. We ask you to open our eyes and when you begin to do that, we close them wide shut.

Father, we have so misrepresented you and your heart, and I'm so sorry. It's one of the reasons, I don't like to identify as a Christian. Enough with the labels. **I'd much rather the fruit of my life speak the volumes of your word.**

It's a heart matter...I'm using those with a heart to be used. No matter what they call themselves.

A DIFFERENT LANGUAGE

Although I went to and was a member of Anglican, Pentecostal and Full Gospel churches, I do not check any boxes for religion on forms, and I do not label myself by denomination. I am just a child of God who believes that the Bible is the Word of God, and He cannot be separated from His word. I try with His help to live by His word, both written and spoken.

That being said, there is a teaching in the Pentecostal Church (which is where it got its name actually) that I'd like to talk about. To properly explain about the teaching, I have to share the biblical account.

When the Day of Pentecost had fully come, they all were in one accord in one place. And suddenly, there came a sound from heaven, as a rushing mighty wind, and it filled the whole house where they were sitting. Then there appeared to them divided tongues, as of fire, and one sat upon each of them. And they were all filled with the Holy Spirit and began to speak with other tongues, as the Spirit gave them utterance. And there were dwelling in Jerusalem Jews, devout men from every nation under heaven. And when this sound occurred, the multitude came together, and were confused because everyone heard them speak in his own language." Acts2:1-7

The teaching is that 'Speaking in Tongues' is the 'initial evidence' that someone is filled with the Holy Spirit. Well, I have found that substantiated nowhere in scripture, so I don't believe it. If ever there was a man-made doctrine, in my mind, this would fit the bill. In addition, it has not been my experience, and I believe that there's a reason why it happened that way at that time. There was a practical reason for different tongues in that scenario.

The above account explains that on the Day of Pentecost when the Holy Spirit came, the people spoke in tongues. In Acts 19:6 those filled with the Holy Spirit spoke in tongues and prophesied. Nothing says that when one is filled, one will always speak in tongues, or that it is any initial evidence of anything.

A lecturer in the Bible School I went to was teaching on the Book of Acts, and she said, "If you're not speaking in tongues, you're not filled with the Holy Ghost. I don't care what anyone says." Meanwhile, God was waking me up and speaking to me prophetically through the Word, but by her teaching, I was not filled with the Holy Ghost.

Anything God had for me, I wanted it, so naturally I prayed, and prayed and prayed for Him to fill me, so I could speak in tongues. I went through an entire range of thoughts and emotions about not being able to speak in tongues. Primarily, this was used in the Church Matrix as some sort of measure that you were actually walking in close relationship with the Lord.

There were churches that would not allow you to 'be in ministry' unless you were spirit-filled, meaning you spoke in tongues. As a result, there were many people who loved the Lord and wanted to serve, but did not make the grade by man's standard.

I experienced the feeling of not being spiritual enough or not loving the Lord enough. I thought that maybe, I was doing something wrong, and eventually, I just resigned myself to "Tongues aren't for me." If I was supposed to have that gift, then God would give it to me in His timing.

Let's look at what the word has to say about tongues.

1. *Mark 16:17 And these signs will accompany those who believe: In my name, they will…speak in new tongues*

2. *I Corinthians 14:2 For anyone who speaks in a tongue does not speak to people, but to God. Indeed, no one understands them; they utter mysteries by the Spirit*

3. *I Corinthians 14:23 So, if the whole church comes together and everyone speaks in tongues, and inquirers or unbelievers come in, will they not say that you are out of your mind?*

4. *I Corinthians 14:27-28 If anyone speaks in a tongue, two or at the most three should speak, one at a time, and someone must interpret. If there is no interpreter, the speaker should keep quiet in the church and speak to himself and God*

5. *I Corinthians 12:8-11 To one there is given through the Spirit a message of wisdom, to another a message of knowledge by means of the same Spirit…to another speaking in different kinds of tongues, and to still another, the interpretation of tongues. All*

these are the work of one and the same Spirit, and He distributes them to each one just as He determines

6. *I Corinthians 13:1 If I speak with the tongues of men or of angels, but do not have love, I am only a resounding gong or a clanging cymbal*

7. *I Corinthians 14:2 For anyone who speaks in a tongue does not speak to people, but to God. Indeed, no one understands them.*

Tongues are a gift, and the Holy Spirit distributes gifts to us as He sees fit.

Tongues shouldn't be spoken in church unless there is an interpretation, something to this day, I have never experienced. Perhaps, it came forth as a prophetic word after the tongues were spoken, but it was never stated. I am not in a position to say.

Tongues are a prayer language…a way to allow the Holy Spirit to pray through us

The account in Acts shows a very practical use as well. It's a way for God to communicate His message through His people who may not know a foreign language to people who speak that language.

MY EXPERIENCE

As I stated before, I don't believe that the gift of tongues is any yardstick to judge whether someone is filled with the Holy Spirit or not. I think this teaching only serves to put people in a box and cause them unnecessary heartache.

However, the word says,

If a son shall ask bread of any of you that is a father, will he give him a stone? Or if he asks a fish, will he for a fish give him a serpent? Or if he shall ask an egg, will he offer him a scorpion? If you then being evil know how to give good gifts unto your children: how much more shall your heavenly Father give the Holy Spirit to them that ask Him? Luke 11:11-13

Many years ago, I was in a church service that was geared toward getting people 'filled with the Holy Spirit,' but really to 'speak in tongues.' There was a teaching and then, a call was made for people who wanted to 'be filled' to come up.

So, I went up because I was desirous of speaking in tongues, even though I believed I was already filled with the Holy Spirit. As the lady got to me, I said to her that I didn't believe that tongues had anything to do with being filled. She said to me, "Ok, but you need it." There was no argument there from me because I did believe that tongues as a prayer language was a 'good gift' for me to have.

She prayed with me and told me to open my mouth and begin to speak in faith. I did, and to my surprise, I was speaking in tongues.

Before this experience, I had a misconception that tongues would just come upon me and override my will, and I'd have no control over my utterances. This is not so. Although, I can choose when and where I speak in tongues, my brain is not involved in what comes out of my mouth.

This is the part that really helps in my prayer life, as sometimes, I just don't know what I should pray. Holy Spirit does that through tongues on my behalf.

About four years ago, I 'bounced up' my friend in the mall with three of her Venezuelan friends. She is bilingual, but they were not. I sat with them for a while and she was telling me about what their plight was and asked me to pray for them.

It was impressed upon me to pray for them in tongues. Somewhere in my being, I believed that they would be able to understand me. So, I asked my friend to explain to them what I was going to do, and they consented.

When I prayed for them, my friend did not understand a thing I had said, neither did two of the men. One of the men did though. He was able to say to her in Spanish what I had prayed, and she told me in English what he had heard. (It occurred to me recently, that maybe, he had the gift of 'Interpretation of Tongues,' but that's just me making connections again.) Had I prayed in English though, it was what I would have most likely prayed.

Today, I still pray in tongues, and from my observation, I speak in several different languages (none of which sound like any of the tongues I've heard). This has been an invaluable gift to me in my prayer life, as Holy Spirit prays on target. I do not yet interpret though, but this is a gift that I've asked God for as I'd like to know what I'm saying.

I've had some thoughts about my experience as it relates to 'Speaking in Tongues.' I believe that God doesn't withhold good things from us, and if He does, He has a very good reason.

When I used to pray and pray for it to happen, it never did. I think that motive played a role in why I didn't receive it then. In my heart, I had attached some sort of validation of my relationship with God and my self- worth to being able to speak in tongues. I also believe He wanted me to 'believe right.' If tongues had anything to do with being filled, then I would have been speaking in tongues from the day I was saved.

When I had let go of the 'need,' it happened, and also at a time when I had come to a different understanding of it. I think the fact that the lady didn't 'fight me down,' and she empowered me to speak by faith made a huge difference in my receiving the gift.

In fact, when she instructed me to speak, it was as though she had said to me, "It has been given. You already have it. Open it up." I acted on it by faith because I believed that I had already received it.

CHURCH OUT THE BOX

I grew up attending the Anglican Church and did First Communion and Confirmation. My mom sent me to Sunday-School and service even when she wasn't going herself. I've always felt different…like there must be something more to this walk with God, especially as it related to the supernatural.

I'm thankful for the foundation in Christ that my Mom gave me, as I have returned to it. She would read and pray with me as a child at bedtime, and she always talked to me. More importantly, she walked out His character before me. I've always believed in God, and I've always spoken to Him. I knew He was real, and I knew He cared about me.

I didn't connect with church as I'd known it though, and as soon as I could stop going, I did. I left Trinidad when I was sixteen to go to school in Canada, and that marked the end of attending traditional church and the beginning of my spiritual exploration. I never stopped praying though, and I could see the hand of God on my life. I used to pray for Him to show me His truth. I can't say that I was living for Him then though. I just tried to be 'good,' but I lived a life 'in the world.'

I remember a conversation with a friend of mine at high school about relationship with God and how it's not about being a good person, but being born again. That made no sense to me at the time. I remember another incident in class when a girl stood up and said, "If you're not serving Jesus, you're going to hell." That was so offensive to me at the time, and I thought that she was so ignorant and disrespectful. How could she say that? "Every person will get to heaven through their own religion," I said. As a Christian, I know now that view is contrary to what God says in His Word.

I've said all of this to give you a picture of my background. I knew that the supernatural world was very real and that we could do extraordinary and powerful things. This was the source of my searching which led me into the world of New Age and the Occult. I didn't delve as deeply as I could have, but I did enough to be able to recognise the Truth when I encountered it. I could never reconcile some things with the foundation in Christ that I had been given.

When I returned to Trinidad, I returned with some 'books' and my tarot cards. These disturbed my mother, and I know she used to pray for me. I got a job with a wholesale company doing direct sales and merchandising. This job took me throughout the country and to St. Vincent and Grenada where I trained sales representatives. I learnt a lot about people and God on the field, and I had some strange and unforgettable encounters. This job brought out the worst and best in me.

God knows how to draw every one of us to Himself, and He did so with me in such a personal and undeniable way. I was led on a path that brought me to a church in Marabella one day, where I discovered that the pastor was my cousin. We had not been in touch for many years, and I never knew that he was pastoring a church. He invited me to church, and I promised him that I would visit one day. I shared when I returned to the office with a friend of mine who promised that he would go with me. When I got home, I shared the happening with my mom, and told her that I would go that Sunday.

Sunday morning came, and I was getting ready to go when it started raining. So, I suggested that perhaps, I shouldn't go, but mom insisted. By the time, I was ready to leave the house, it stopped raining. Hmm...

I arrived at church very early, not even the ushers were there. I spoke to my cousin briefly, and he seated me reassuring me that someone would be along soon. It's very strange how I never had a thought about leaving, but stayed till the very end...and what an end it was.

There is no doubt in my mind that God orchestrated everything for me to be there that day. It seemed as though the entire sermon was just for me. It was as though God Himself was speaking to me about things only He and I knew about.

To think that this God loved me despite all those things in my life, and He, Jesus wanted a relationship with me, even though I denied Him. I sat there in tears, snot running down my nose. When that alter call was made for surrendering my life to Jesus, I got up from my seat and walked straight up to the altar. That day, I was 'born again.'

I grew very quickly in the Word, and I had an insatiable desire to read the Bible, and its nuggets opened up for me. I understood it easily, even in ancient English. I received the Word and instruction with childlike faith because I knew that God had brought me to this point. I even had about three semesters of Bible School where I started an Associate Degree in Theology.

I knew I had to burn those tarot cards (which resisted fire and gas. They took a very long time to burn when they finally ignited.) and I tried to retrieve the Wicca books from an ex of mine to burn them. I think he didn't believe that I was going to burn them, so he didn't give them to me.

I did resist things like 'doh party' and 'doh drink' though because I didn't see anything wrong with them. I said to the Lord that if He wanted me to stop those things that He'd have to tell me Himself. Sure enough, He did through a specific sign I had asked for and I obeyed. I had a heart for the Lord, and I knew that He pursued me and brought me to the knowledge of His Truth. My searching was over, but I desired to know Him better.

Nothing used to turn me off more than when people would ask, "Do you know Jesus? Are you a Christian?" It seemed impersonal and like it was a recruiting campaign that held no genuine concern for me. I never wanted to become one of 'those people.'

Prior to my encounter with the Lord through salvation, it made no sense saying to me that the Bible or word of God says such and such because I did not yet have a revelation that the Bible was His inspired word. One can however, say or show through one's life and relationship what God says and show His nature and character. People can read the epistle of our lives, as they may never step foot in a church or read the bible.

"By this, all will know that you are My disciples, if you have love for one another." John 13:35

With salvation, I was back to 'church,' not the kind I was used to. I've done all sorts of church, church in a school, church upstairs KFC, potluck dinner church in a home, bible-study tea time, church in a rum factory where I could wear jeans and sit on the lawn with my baby, church under an old, abandoned house, church with club ambiance, cult church, church retreat and apostolic/prophetic church, woman pastor church, people pushing you down church, you name it, I've probably had an experience with it.

You would think I was searching ***ent?*** I suppose, I've been to many 'small churches' as they say here about Pentecostal, Full Gospel and Bible Believing churches because I've moved a lot both within Trinidad and Tobago and other islands. There are some that I just visited and there are some that I was a 'member' or 'covenant partner' of. There was one that I preached at. I've never left any of the ones I was committed to unless I'd been instructed by God to do so, even when I saw things I didn't agree with or did not want to tolerate...I've always had a meeting with pastors when exiting and in most cases written a formal letter.

I've been accused of church-hopping, I've been called rebellious, I've been lied on from the pulpit, I've been accused of trying to be super-spiritual because I had faith that the pastor should have had and I've been stabbed in the back by 'friends' for favour with pastor. If there's one thing I know is how to stand with God alone.

I've always understood that I am the church, the body of Christ, and there is just ONE church of Jesus Christ. Different parts of the body may meet in different places, but there is no division or denomination in God's church. There's no Pastor Smith's church and Father John's church or Apostle Jane's church. There's no Catholic church or Methodist church or Adventist church...not according to the Bible I've read.

Why am I required to join something that I already became when I surrendered to Christ? I love God and I love 'the church,' comprising my brothers and sisters in Christ, who I fellowship with regularly in different ways and in different places. They aren't limited to any one denomination. What I do have an issue with is manipulation, keeping people dependent and stifling their growth, fleecing the flock and using money in maintaining and building structures while people starve or don't have a home or support.

Every part of the body has its issues and no place on earth is heaven. I've learnt to take what I need and leave the rest until God moves me. The devil loves to have us offended and tied up in confusion that we tune out from what God is trying to do. Some pastors genuinely believe that what they're teaching and doing is the right thing because it's what they were taught and they've operated within that paradigm. Their hearts are in the right place; I don't hold it against them.

There's a whole system and structure set up to support it, and those who operate within that 'matrix' seldom deviate because it would mean ostracism or coming down from that elevated *platform on* which they've been placed. In my mind, it's a question of misplaced identity. It's not fun to be standing alone, but God says we must not love anyone more than Him, not even our own parents. We should not have fear for what anyone can do to us. (Ref. Matthew 10:27-31)

As such, the word of God is sometimes compromised because of obligation. The flow of the spirit is stifled, and breakthrough hindered because of men's agendas. 'Ministry' or service to God is relegated to 'certain activities' and what is done within the walls of the organisation, and people's commitment to God is measured by how much time they devote to the organisation and within the walls.

My view of ministry is far broader. It's about being who my Heavenly Father wants me to be and doing what He wants me to do, wherever He has me. Ministry is about using what He's placed in me to bring Him glory. My business is ministry, for who I am ties into what I do. Therefore, living out purpose is ministry. Writing this book is ministry, hugging someone is ministry, marriage is ministry and showing unconditional love is ministry. I aspire to live my life as an act of worship and service.

I used to ask God why He moved me around the way He did, both in my abode and in my fellowship spaces. I wanted to be settled, but I'm very appreciative for all the experiences I've had and all that I've learnt. I think I have a unique perspective.

I want to formally thank all the men and women of God who have sown into me, but as my friend Nicole says, "I say things that nobody else will say." I suppose it's because I've stood alone so much for Christ's sake that I'm obligated to no one. I have no title or status to lose, and all that I have and am is because of Him. As long as I know what He's said and I'm in His will, I'm good because ultimately, He's been my only source.

My walk with Him has been such that I've had to trust Him and not what my circumstances looked like, even to the point of appearing foolish at times. And so, it continues...

"And whatever you do, do it heartily, as to the Lord and not to men, knowing that from the Lord you will receive the reward of the inheritance; for you serve the Lord Christ."
Colossians 3:23-24

LIFE IN THE 'CHURCH MATRIX'

These are some of the realities that happen in the church matrix or religious system.

- Five-fold ministers are above correction or cannot be questioned unless you hold a title or position of like or above. (I'm not speaking here about trying to show someone up in public. That's out of order.)

- The view is held that God can't speak to people in the congregation before He speaks to them. God would tell them everything and show them what's going on in their congregation. As such, they rob themselves of much needed guidance. Why can't God show them through someone? On the flip side, there are those who befriend the flock in a way that encourages people to bring news about other members. Then they stand on the pulpit and say that God showed them such and such. The word actually says that we see in part and we know in part. I think it is for this very reason...that we could get puffed up. So, He's made us interdependent. (Even the 'donkey' has a message. We often miss it because we don't regard the messenger as being worthy. God is no respecter of persons)

- If, you 'buy in' to service and commitment to God equating with all your time, energy and finances being 'tied up' in the organisation, then there will be little or no time for recreation, family, friends or even pursuing your purpose or true ministry. God never meant for us to be burnt out or all work and no play. In some extreme cases, 'church events' will be planned for any holidays or time off that could otherwise be spent away from church and 'church people'

- Often, a case of misplaced identity can cause us to 'people please' or 'pastor please' because there's a fear of rejection or not being seen as spiritual… there's a need for a sense of belonging. The church then becomes a social club or a 'friendly society.' Often, people stay when they should leave because they're in an abusive relationship with the church or they are waiting on pastor to recognise them and promote them to a position. If God already validated the call, man doesn't need to

- Anytime, there is a suspicion or threat of a member leaving, a position would be dangled in front of them, or a guilt trip placed on them, "Oh, we were just about to make you…" or "There are so many people looking at you, how would this affect them?"

- If 'Pastor' didn't say it, it's not true or valid, and in extreme cases, Pastor's permission or sanction needs to be sought for most life decisions. (I'm not speaking here of seeking godly counsel, but of dependency and an inability to make decisions without first consulting Pastor)

- If you know who you are and don't accept or agree with whatever box a leader is trying to put you in, then you'll be labelled as rebellious or told you have a problem with submission. In most cases, you'll be side-lined

- Pastor, Prophet, Apostle or whoever comes to minister will deliver a message that speaks to 'goings on' in the church having been fully apprised. This is not always God's message to the house.

It's sad when those who have titles and positions of authority don't heed the leading of the Lord through those they perceive to be less than or know less than them. This is the beauty about God, He's no respecter of persons, and He's given more honour to the uglier body parts and those that are unseen, 1 Cor. 12:23 and He uses the foolish things to put to shame the wise, so none of us could glory in ourselves.
(1 Cor. 1:27)

If He could cause a donkey to talk, why wouldn't He use anyone or anything He can to get a message to us? In I Kings 13, we see an account of a young prophet losing his life from disobedience to the Lord by listening to an older prophet who had actually lied to him. He was forewarned by God not to listen to any other instruction but the one He had given him- even if it was an older prophet.

Some things only have value within the matrix and seek to serve it. It has a culture all of its own. In the world outside of that culture, there is no significance or relevance. The irony is that the world outside is who the church is supposed to be impacting.

If we could only see things in terms of what God said and not position and status, the world would be a much better place. We are told to not think of ourselves more highly than we ought.

The moral of all this is simple:

Know and hear God for yourselves...He speaks to all of us and desires intimate relationship with all of us. None of us earned to right to be any closer to God than anyone else.

For by grace you have been saved through faith, and not of yourselves; it is a gift of God, not of works, lest anyone should boast. For we are His workmanship, created in Christ Jesus for good works, which God prepared beforehand that we should walk in them. Ephesians 2: 8-10

THE COVERING

Many pastors replace God as 'spiritual covering' in their congregations. Some people believe the word of a human being over the word of God because they think that someone with the title somehow hears God better than them or knows God more.

There are some who will not 'hear' until Pastor or Prophet says. This is further exacerbated by the said leaders teaching about 'spiritual covering' and that someone who is not a member of 'established organisation' (because you can't just attend any one either) is not under authority. Therefore, what he/she has to say is worth nothing. It is so easy for people who genuinely love the Lord to be manipulated when they don't know Him for themselves.

Don't get me wrong, I believe that there is a role for five-fold ministers (Apostle, Prophet, Teacher, Preacher, Evangelist) to teach, nurture and edify the body into maturity; however, their role should not interfere with the *free will* of individuals or cause them to be dependent on them for their guidance and instruction. A relationship with God is what should be encouraged, and learning to hear His voice for themselves.

> *"My sheep hear My voice, and I know them, and they follow Me." John 10:27*

In the world of 'Churchianity,' those who are not 'under a covering' or who are not members of an organisation are seen as rebellious, not under authority, not accountable to anyone, not under the anointing, not in order or right standing with God and certainly not in the will of God. Oh, and all these things can also be said if you are part of a congregation with a female pastor at the head, depending on who you talk to.

Need I say that at various times in my life, I would have been labelled one or all of the above. I suppose if I had a desire to belong or to be 'in ting,' I would have been swayed to take a different course of action, other than what I was instructed by God to do.

I think in part that He wanted to disabuse me of people-pleasing and being manipulated, but mostly, He wanted my identity and self-worth to be firmly rooted in Him and Him alone. He wanted me to be governed by faith in Him alone and not tossed ***to and fro*** by emotions and opinions of people.

Would I stand alone in what He said if the whole world was against me? Would I say what He said, even if the older, more experienced 'prophet' did not agree? Would I move forward with the vision He has given me? Would I be more concerned about how I looked or sounded?

It's not uncommon to hear things like, "She walked out from under the anointing; she left before it was God's timing; watch and see, she will never make it; the banana that gets picked, gets eaten." One pastor preached on me for quite some time after I had left. After all, she had the rest of her flock to protect from 'going astray.' If any of these things about me were actually true, shouldn't loving people who care about me have compassion and pray for my best? God's people should.

At the very worst, even if I had said or done things against anyone, on leaving, the response of the church should be:

"But I say to you who hear: Love your enemies, do good to those who hate you, bless those who curse you, and pray for those who spitefully use you." Luke 6:27-28

As children of God, we don't get to be spiteful or vengeful. 'Love covers the multitude of sins.' (I Peter 4:8)

The implication of walking out from 'under the anointing' is that this anointing only resides in them or in their building, but really it's about being under their control and manipulation. In some cases, it's about losing tithes. Is God not with me wherever I go?

The Word tells me,

But the anointing which you have received from Him abides in you, and you do not need that anyone teach you; but as the same anointing teaches you concerning all things, and is true, and is not a lie, and just as it has taught you, you will abide in Him. I John 2:27

But you have an anointing from the Holy One and you know all things. John 2:20

For He Himself said, I will never leave you nor forsake you. Hebrews 13:5

Where can I go from your Spirit? Or where can I flee from Your presence? If I ascend into heaven, You are there; If I make my bed in hell, behold, You are there Psalms 139:7-8

The Lord is near to all who call upon Him, to all who call upon Him in truth. Psalms 145:18

There is a scripture that is often used when people are trying to coerce people back into 'church membership.' It is this, *"not forsaking the assembling of ourselves together, as is the manner of some..." Hebrews 10:25*

The conversation would usually go something like this,
Church Person: "So where do you fellowship?"
Me: "Nowhere right now,"
Church Person: "But you know, we aren't to forsake the assembly?"
Me: "Yes, but the Lord would not have me to be anywhere right now."
Church Person: "Yes, but you know, that covering is important..."

Is the 'covering' of a man or woman superior to that of God, and if every pastor or bishop is under a covering, who covers the person at the top of this pyramid? Does he or she have more access to God than the people below?

"He who dwells in the secret place of the Most-High shall abide under the shadow of the Almighty." Psalms 91:1

Was the death of Christ in vain then?

"There is one God and one mediator between God and man, the Man Christ Jesus." I Timothy 2:5

If we look at the 'forsaking the assembly' scripture again taking into account, what comes before and what follows, my understanding of it is that we are to get together with our brothers and sisters in love to encourage each other in the faith and in doing what God called us to do.

> *"And let us consider one another in order to stir up love and good works, not forsaking the assembling of ourselves together, as is the manner of some, but exhorting one another..." Hebrews 10:24*

If this is so, why should 'our gathering' be limited to a traditional 'place of worship?'

> *"For where two or three are gathered together in My name, I am there in the midst of them." Matthew 18:20*

If the issue of covering is about Accountability, can this not be had with relationships of God's choosing that are not limited to the 'organisation' or the building?

I've been a 'born again' believer now for over twenty years. Before I got saved, God assigned a prophet/mentor to me as a friend who is still in my life. Over the years, He has also placed what I call an 'inner circle' of friends of different ages, and denominations who I very much hold myself accountable to. I love them and trust them, and I know they love me and have my best interest at heart. Most importantly, they love the Lord. They have the permission to speak into my life and to pull me up when they see me going wrong. We pray for each other, and we meet up from time to time (not all at the same time). We share laughter and tears, we sow into each other, financially and otherwise, we support each other's businesses, endeavors and marriages.

Whether I was in or out 'of church,' I was receiving from the Lord and growing in my relationship with Him and others. In fact, in the times I was not in 'a church,' I grew closest to the Lord because I was not tied up in 'activity' and going to the building, but I could spend quality time in the word and talking to Him.

I had to depend on Him even more, and I learnt to hear His voice for myself. In addition, I was free to move about and do as He had instructed me. I can only speak from a place of my experience with God.

I am not knocking church because I do attend when I'm led to, but I'm saying that we should know God for ourselves and understand that we, the body of Christ are the church, and we are called to be that church wherever we are. The church is an organism and not an organisation. I'm saying we should obey God before we obey man. There may be times when this is the same thing.

As new believers, we need to be taught and be in community with a body of believers. The Christian walk is not easy, especially if we don't have enough word deposited in us or if we don't know God that good yet. I view organised church like school. You start at preschool and go all the way up to tertiary. There are tests and promotions and then, one day, we go out into the world to put what we've learnt into practice. We may stop going to school, but we never stop learning, and we would have developed a discipline of self-directed learning and a solid, ongoing relationship.

Isn't that what 'the Great Commission' is all about? We are called to go out into the world, not stick up in the building, and what of those of us who have been called to the marketplace? When do we grow up and get to go out? If we only mingle in Christian circles with Christian people, and we're getting fat on the word, we are failing to fulfill the Great Commission.

> ***The Great Commission***
> *Go into all the world and preach the gospel to every creature. He who believes and is baptised will be saved; but he who does not believe will be condemned. And these signs shall follow those who believe: In My name they will cast out demons: they will speak with new tongues: they will take up serpents: and if they drink anything deadly, it will by no means hurt them: they will lay hands on the sick and they will recover. Mark 16:15-18*

The 'good news' or gospel is about Love…that Christ died for us because He loved us before we ever knew He existed, and that He loved me in my nastiness. He never required anything of me, but to come to Him as I was. He never required me to clean up my act before coming to Him. I could never have done that on my own anyway. He's the cleanup Master.

I said from day one that if I was going to be a follower of Christ that I wanted to be a real one…the kind I read about in the Bible who could heal the sick, raise the dead and who could speak on God's behalf and impact thousands. I wanted to be effective, but when I encountered Him, I most of all wanted to have His heart. Nothing I could do would matter if I don't have love. I wanted people to know and experience what a loving relationship with God is like.

If you're going to church religiously, sitting under the covering and not growing in love and the fruit of the spirit, with no improvement in your life, then perhaps, you need to ask God some serious questions.

If you're sitting under the covering waiting on someone to bestow a title, position or validate your call, before you obey God in doing what Christ spilled precious blood and took blows for you to do, then you need to reevaluate your motives. *"Whatever is not of faith is sin..." Romans 14:23*

If I believed that God was saying to me to commit to another part of the body in the 'church system,' I would do it in obedience, but I'm clear that it is not the path He has for me at this point in time. I do visit churches though, and I remain open to whatever the Lord would have me to do.

In being committed to that part of the body, I would submit myself to the 'Order of the House' (regardless of whether it's oppressive or not) for as long as God requires me to because I believe that He's a God of order.

My stance however is and will always be doing as I believe God has instructed me to, and history with Him has shown that He would not cause me to be a part of an oppressive system or situation forever.

If He has asked me to submit to something for a time, it is for a work He wants to do in me or in that part of the body. It would never be 'in His order' to leave before He has instructed because I don't like things that are being done or I'm offended for some reason.

"Father, if it is Your will, take this cup away from Me; nevertheless, not my will but Yours be done." Luke 22:42

Even if there was something wrong that I could see in leaving, I don't get to hold anything or anyone in my heart. As a child of God, unforgiveness is not an option. Furthermore, I have a responsibility to pray about the situation and for the people involved.

DELIVERANCE

One of the meanings of the word deliverance in its literal sense is to be 'freed or rescued from captivity.' It may also imply being loosed from something into something else.

Without getting spooky or super-spiritual, I'd like to talk about deliverance in a specific context.

Just as we have a physical DNA which continues to be perpetuated throughout the generations after us, so too, we also have a spiritual DNA. Just as the roots of trees determine their fruit (even though they are beneath the surface, and we tend to not see them), in this way, our spiritual DNA/roots determine much of the fruit in our lives.

An example of how this plays out is in our marriages. Many of us may agree that despite our best efforts, we had found ourselves in a marriage situation similar to that of our parents. Our husbands display behaviors our fathers did, or your parents were divorced, and you're divorced etc.

Depending on who you talk to, they may call this by a different name. In the case of sickness, doctors may use the term 'hereditary,' in the case of abuse, psychologists may term it 'the cycle of abuse,' in Christianity, it is termed 'generational curses.'

We will attract to ourselves whatever is in us, therefore, the way to secure a 'better future' is to be DELIVERED. We need to be loosed from generational bondage. Often, we tend to see undesirable behavior in others while remaining blind to our own. We may say, "I would never do…" However, there are things that we would do. What I'm trying to say is this: The root is the same, even though the manifestation of the fruit may appear to be different.

It's like magnets. In essence, the magnets are made up of the same stuff; however, there is a negative pole and a positive pole. The opposites attract, but they both still remain magnets. In order for us to stop attracting the 'wrong,' our spiritual DNA needs to be changed.

Deliverance is what is necessary. Deliverance is not necessarily a one-time thing, but involves 'work' on our parts in complete co-operation and surrender to God. **Deliverance is an act of the will**. Ask Him to show you the junk in you that needs to come out, (focusing less on the faults in others) and be prepared to take action where necessary and to do some things differently. It is so important to take the time with God to 'do the work' or we'll be doomed to repeat our mistakes or attract the same elements to our lives.

Deliverance is essential for coming 'Out the Box.'

FASTING...NOT A FAS' TING

This kind can come out by nothing, but prayer and fasting. Mark 9:29

Deliverance is not always a 'fas' ting' like many pastors would have you believe. You don't need anyone to lay hands on you, or pour 'holy' water and recite a bunch of prayers. There are times when it can happen this way, but for most, I think deliverance happens by a process involving the surrendering of the will, prayer and fasting.

For strongholds and generational issues, our souls (mind, will and emotions) must be crucified or surrendered to the will of God. This is what is meant by dying to the flesh.

A fast is not only about staying away from food and drink, but in my experience, it may also include abstinence from the thing that 'so easily besets.' For example, if I'm a smoker, staying away from food and drink while continuing to smoke is not going to deliver me from that addiction. That seems absurd right?

Equally absurd is the expectation that a person will stay free if there's no BIG reason to do so...something that drives that person to stay clean on a heart level. A change of heart or repentance is necessary.

I've had the opportunity to go to a few Narcotics Anonymous meetings recently. I've also visited another Rehab Centre, and I've had a working relationship with U-Turn for Christ. My mind makes connections and draws parallels.

All of these organisations concern themselves with the recovery and or rehabilitation of addicts. The first phase in live-in recovery programmes is detox or abstinence where clients must not 'Use' or 'Indulge' in any drug (or any mind altering or habit-forming substance) or habit (gambling, internet, devices, porn) for a specified number of days, without contact with anyone on the outside. In essence, this is a fast.

While on this fast and throughout the programme, there is a 'renewing of the mind' through drama, the Word, experiential learning, other readings and counselling. There must be an exposure of brokenness and a willful exchanging of old thoughts and mindsets for those that are life giving, productive and empowering.

Prayer (talking to God) is also enjoined in whatever form it may take. This is a common and essential component of any recovery programme...a directing of clients to forging a relationship with Almighty God. It is said that the most critical thing in recovery is for clients to know that they are loved. This is the cement that holds everything together. Dare I say, this is the foundation of their freedom... knowing that they are loved.

I've concluded that for deliverance or freedom from bondage to be complete, it must address individuals on three levels, body, soul and spirit.

Love, however is the most powerful force in the universe, and He has the power to heal the broken hearted, fill every void and transform the hardest of persons. God is love, and freedom and transformation come when we encounter His love.

MY DELIVERANCE STORY

When I was going through my separation, there was an overseas, online relationship that I had forged (not a random person). I was quite consumed with him, and were we not in separate countries, this relationship may have become actually and not virtually sexual.

I recognised that it was already inappropriate for me because (1) I was still married (although separated) and (2) It should not have gotten to the places that it had already gone. I began to struggle because God had told me to sever it because I was still married 'in the eyes of God and man.' In addition, it really would have been trouble with a capital 'T' if he had come to Trinidad and we had met. I was not supposed to be having sexual relations with anyone except my husband.

So, I prayed and asked God to help him to understand why we just couldn't.

Let me say that I thought I loved this man. He told me everything that I wanted to hear. He 'touched' all the right buttons, but I had been so emotionally starved in my marriage, it seemed like I'd struck an oasis.

God said, "Go on a fast." More than any desire, I wanted to please the Lord, so I obeyed. Initially, I thought the fast was for him, but soon understood that the fast was for me. On this fast, I had no meat and no flour in addition to no connection with the individual. Did he try to communicate? Yes, but I did not respond. This was extremely hard for me, especially since, he didn't 'do anything wrong.'

I really fought through those feelings about what he must think about me. He must have thought I was weird or crazy.

I still had a need for people to view me as 'a nice person,' and I believe God wanted to purge me of that. I decided that I cared more about what God thought, so I died a little each day.

When I started this fast, I didn't know how long it was going to be for, and just went one day at a time. It turns out that it was forty days when it had ended. About two weeks into the fast, I'd noticed my stomach swelling. So much so that my friend asked me what was going on because my stomach looked high.

Then, one afternoon after work, I began to have what felt like contractions. By the time I got home, I was struck with a sharp pain that ran from my stomach down to my groin. I could only say the name of Jesus as I lay down on the bed. That pain passed after a few minutes, but I was concerned about what had caused the pain and the swelling.

I tried to get the names and numbers of gynecologists who would be able to see me on short notice to no avail. The next morning, I made a few phone calls…still futile and I was not about the pay $600…just didn't have it. A friend had told me to treat with it in the spirit because treating with it in the natural alone would not deal with the root.

I called in to work 'sick,' and I decided to deal with this whole scenario spiritually. As I sat on my bed, He said to me through the Bible account in Mark 9, "This kind only comes out by prayer and fasting." It occurred to me that the boy in the story had the issue from birth which said to me that it was a generational issue and that I had to treat with it by renouncing and calling out all the evils that I knew were a part of my lineage.

So, that's exactly how I spent my day…between sitting on my bed and sitting on the toilet as I cast out everything I could think of. Every time I called out the sin, I would have a stomach gripe and have to run to the toilet. This went on for the entire day until it was time to leave to get my son.

After this experience happened, I observed that my need to be communicating with the individual no longer existed. There was no pull. A few days after the fast was over, he was in Trinidad and he called me using a different phone number. I told him that I could not apologise for doing what God asked me to do. He was still saying to me that we could probably meet for coffee sometime, to which I refused.

God had to remove the common ground in me that was attracting the same kind of man…but I was so blinded by the lust that I could not see or think straight.

This is how I know that deliverance is also an act of the will…a willingness to surrender what I think I want for what God says. Lust is lust. It's not just a sexual thing. We can lust (have an intense desire) for anything that is against the will of God.

BRAIN MATTER VS. HEART MATTER

We can know about God in our minds and still not yet know Him in our hearts. The encounter in our hearts is what brings transformation. If we aren't healed in our hearts, we won't be open enough for others to experience His heart through us.

Doesn't this mean that there is the potential to get hurt? Certainly. Didn't Jesus choose to come to earth even though He knew He'd be rejected? By giving us free-will, God actually gave us the power to reject or hurt Him.

God wants us to love the way He does...unconditionally. This is how the world will encounter His heart. First, we must be willing to open our own hearts to Him, so that He can come in and heal all the broken places. We must open up all the chambers of our heart to His love. We can't give to others what we don't have. The thing is to know that our emotions are safe with Him.

How we perceive God will determine how we relate to Him and what we access from Him. Knowing God is a heart matter. When we know Him, then we trust Him in spite of what we see, feel or even think. There are times when even the thoughts flowing through our minds can cause us great distress when they don't reflect His heart.

The difference between knowing about God in our heads, and knowing Him in our hearts is as the difference between living our lives with God in it, asking Him to bless it and living our lives for God.

That difference is the difference between being led by the spirit and being led by the flesh. 'Those who are led by the

Spirit are the sons of God.' (Romans 8:14) Being spirit led is a heart posture. When our hearts have been postured to please Him and do His will, then our steps shall be ordered and all things will work together for our good.

What is not of faith is sin because it's not coming from a heart that trusts Him, and therefore self-effort.

The Father is calling us to a place of knowing Him, His heart posture towards us and towards others. The implication here is that even when we see things that seem contrary to what He said or when we don't understand what is happening, we know that He loves us. We must know that His heart is for us and therefore, all His thoughts concerning us are good. That being said, love is not always warm and cushy. Sometimes, it's hard and downright uncomfortable, for Jesus is both the Lion and the Lamb.

THE HEART OF WAR

At the heart of all our negative behavior is fear of something and self-centeredness. If we can become aware of what it is and displace it with faith, we can break free and come out of our boxes. Some things are assigned to us because of our 'call.' More so, because of our prophetic voice.

The prophet hears God and speaks on His behalf, brings words to others to warn, set free, activate, exhort, encourage, and comfort.

If the enemy can get us to doubt our identity and feel like a nobody, like we're not good enough, or too emotional, or don't hear God or whatever contrary to what God says about us, he can stifle our purpose, our voice and by extension hinder what God wants to do through us.

Pride cannot fight pride. Pride's root is self-centeredness born out of fear. Although, what pride incites is for us to protect ourselves, children of God should have no self to protect because we should already be dead. Christ is our defense.

> *"I have been crucified with Christ. It is no longer I who live, but Christ who lives in me. So, I live in this earthly body by trusting in the Son of God who loved me and gave Himself for me." Galatians 2:20*

So, the only thing to fight pride is humility, not self-defense. As we know, we are loved unconditionally by God, we can REST in Him and humble ourselves under His mighty hand. He can then fight on our behalf and lift us up. He is a God of order, so we must submit, but not to the human beings in question, or we will be resentful, especially when they don't mirror His love or hurt our feelings.

Our surrender is only unto man as we are doing it unto God. It must be clear in our minds that submission is unto God, His will. So, we don't do it as a victim, but in the knowledge that it pleases Him and that He loves us and has the final say. Romans 8:37 In this way, He can show off in and through our situations.

It is a privilege and painful pleasure to surrender to the will of God by laying my life down as an act of worship, as He did for me. Resurrection power cannot be made manifest in a vessel that's alive.

God's love never fails, and it does not seek itself. It asks of us to love without exception and expectation, but we can't give what we do not have. Hence, our reliance on the Source for our love and fulfilment.

It's difficult when those who are closest to us are the ones who hurt us the deepest. It's painful and lonely when they don't see our heart or when they don't see the truth of a matter. **We aren't called to be right, only righteous before God, so there's no need to be persuasive, only humble and loving.**

In the case of marriage, a wife must submit to her husband's leading as the head, even if she is right or has been given an instruction by God. In submitting to His order, He will move to bring about His will. We aren't responsible for the outcome if we have given our input, and our husbands decide otherwise. My handling of these situations goes something like this, "Well God, I tried, but your son didn't listen. I place that in your capable hands, and I'm going his way because You said I should submit."

Submission is not being a doormat, it's a powerful strategic position of reliance on the Power of all Powers.

I've seen it so many times where I didn't contend with man and ran to Daddy, and He dealt with the person's heart, often resulting in an apology, different course of action or a change of heart in short order.

The Heart of War is submission to the will of God. The heart of war is love...

YEAH, I LOVE GOD, BUT...

Sometimes, we treat God like a person on the side that we can't be seen with in public...a 'side ting.'

Therefore, everyone who confesses me before men, I will also confess him before My Father who is in heaven. But whoever denies Me before men, I will also deny him before My Father who is in heaven.
Matthew 10:32-33

When you love someone,
Don't you want more of that person?
Don't you want to spend more time with?
When you know that someone cares for you,
Doesn't your love become more intense?
When you truly love that someone,
Doesn't there come a time
When you want to be ONE?
Doesn't there come a time
When you want the world to know
That you belong to each other?
So, how can we love God and keep it a secret?
How can we be ashamed of a love so pure?
How can we keep Him on the down-low?
When He has loved us enough
To suffer public shame and humiliation
And give His life for us?

He wants all of us, for He expects no less than He gave. There was a time when I was ashamed for people to know that I was a Jesus Lover. After all, I used to be one of those people who described them as fanatic.

The truth is, I owe Him my life. When I reflect on the person I used to be and the person I've become, I'm in awe and gratitude. How could He love me in that state, knowing what He knew about me, my thoughts, my nastiness? How could Jesus go through what He went through unto death because He loved me?

I don't know where I would have been were it not for the love of God. I see now any shame that I had was because I hadn't yet given over my life. I'd cared about what other people thought of me more than I cared about what My Father said about me.

It was self-consciousness grounded in fear-the fear of rejection, the fear of not being considered somebody worthwhile, the fear of not having favour and resources. I hadn't yet come to the realization that only God is my Source for everything that I would ever need, and His opinion is the one that matters most. He and I are a majority.

Consequently, I'm not dependent on human beings for my survival, and I hold people and scenarios lightly. There is a liberation that comes from placing trust in God alone. This is not to say that we are not all interdependent, but ultimately, it is God who is able to provide all that we need, and it is He who moves on the hearts of people to favour us.

God never created us to be an island or one-man-show, a body needs different parts to function effectively, but everything starts in the Head.

IT'S ALL A HEART MATTER

*o you remember when you wanted to spend some time alone with him and people kept interrupting how you felt?*
That's the way I feel every time I want to spend time with you and the phone rings, or you're in front of the television.
It hurts when you choose television over me for hours on end. It hurts when you share with everyone else what's going on in your life, or when I'm the last one you ask, "What do you think?" It hurts when they don't share my heart about you.
I love you in a way they never could. Yet, it seems like you value their opinions more than mine. I get jealous because I love you so passionately and deeply. Every thought I have about you is great. I so desire to shower you with my love, to tell you my secrets and to nurture you into that person I created you to be.
Come away with me...meeting in the living room or secret place...there's a flow that happens in the secret place. Just like a lover, I don't always want to speak with you with everyone around. There are things I want to say to only you. There are intimate moments I want to share with only you. I want to share my heart, my love.

It's hard to imagine that You love all of us like this, yet this is the truth.

It's all a heart matter...

Lord, help me to see my heart condition. I know that if you're not first, nothing else will go according to your will, and if I try to hold on to anything or anyone else before you, I'll lose him or it anyway. I know you're a jealous God, and that I'll never truly be happy apart from you. Please help me never to take your love for granted, and draw me deeper into your heart. I want to know your secrets, your thoughts, your plans. I feel off balance when I don't spend enough alone time with you. I miss our times together, and I want our hearts to beat as one, I desire for you to see yourself in me.

Please give me a heart like yours because this is the heart of the matter.

Then I will give them one heart, and I will put a new spirit within them, and take the stony heart out of their flesh, and give them a heart of flesh, that they may walk in My statutes and keep My judgments and do them; and they shall be My people, and I will be their God. Ezekiel 11: 19-20

A PICTURE OF LOVE

I commissioned Prophetic Artist, Natasha Rampersad to do three paintings for the wall of my coaching space. Without saying a word to her, this is one of them, entitled Love. Unbeknown to her was that God would be doing a healing work and opening the chambers of my own heart and drawing me to a place of deeper intimacy with Him. God used her and her artistic gift to speak His heart directly to me. The painting came before He had begun 'the work' for this book.

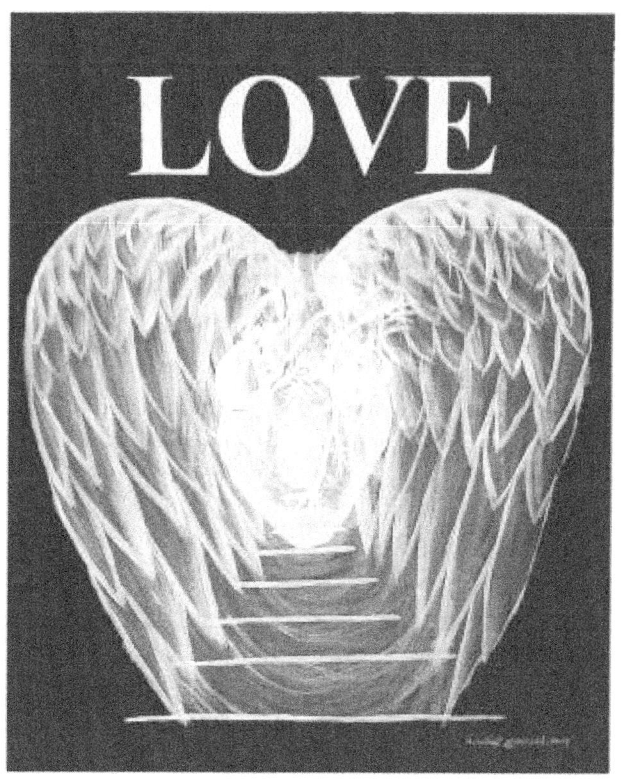

JILL OUT THE BOX-VOL. 2 (Preview)

...MARRIAGE AND MONEY MATTERS (WORKING TITLE)

MANIFESTATION

Many years ago, I think it was 2012, the Lord said to me that JOTBox is a Publishing Company. I accepted His word but had no clue about the how to...only believing that He'd equip me.

I did however purchase a book on Self -Publishing online and started reading. As it turned out, I had already done most of the set up. I never finished that book.

Over the years, JOTBox had been doing all the other written expression things, but no books yet. I've received many words about the many books I would publish.

Fast forward to 2020, I'm finally finished writing my book and getting ready to publish. In my thinking, I should go through the process first with my book before I do anyone else's.

An opportunity came up to publish a book for someone in January with a 'soft launch' on January 31st, 2020. I tried all how to get out of it believing that the time was too short, thinking I was doing my own book among other things...

It's amazing how things happen sometimes when God wants you to do something. We had less than three weeks, but I'm here to report that JOTBox just published its first book entitled, "Broken But Beautiful- A Struggle with Lupus and Journey For a Kidney Transplant," an Autobiography by Dr. Jacqueline Deon Simmonds Goulbourne. She says that she knew that JOTBox was the Publisher to work with her, and I'm so grateful that God gave us both the opportunity.

As this was a first-fruit book, I did not charge what I should have for the work involved (I believe that the Lord gave me a figure), however He moved on the author's heart to pay me more than I had asked for. In addition, she also flew Chilo and me to Jamaica so that I could speak at the launch.

If someone had said to me that I would have been in Jamaica at the beginning of the year, I would have said, "Nah, I doubt," but God...I never saw it coming.

We stayed at the University of the West Indies, Mona Visitor's Lodge, so Chilo got a sample of campus life. We still got to do a few leisure things. The launch went well, and I was approached by two other people about doing their stories.

If I had gone My way, there would have been no Jamaica trip or other open doors. That being said, I still paid a price to complete this project. *(Just because God is in something, it doesn't mean that we'll never have any challenges or trials, but He promises to bring us through all of them and work all things together for our good.)*

If He said it, He'll do it. I got a crash course in Publishing. The week after returning from Jamaica, another person with a book showed up on my doorstep. It has begun...

SOMETHING OLD, SOMETHING FLU

Who knew that in March 2020 our country would be on lock down because of a world pandemic called COVID-19. I'll tell you who knew, God did, and none of this is a surprise to Him. This is not to be insensitive or naive, but there are many positives I see as it relates to our current COVID-19 state of affairs.

1. God has been trying to do a 'new thing' for some time now. COVID-19 has forced the church out of the buildings and into homes and communities. The real church now has to 'stand up'

2. We are in a transition. This is a transformational opportunity for us as a people, a nation, region, the world. When it boils down to it, we are all human and none of us are exempt from the impact of COVID-19 in one way or another. Will be pull together? Will we utilise our resources well, will we come into our true purposes? Some of us have not exercised our faith to leave that job or to shift to that different thing, now it has been forced upon many

3. Our leaders can operate in a way that serves the people and should be commended and supported

4. There is no creed, race, high class, low class, colour, nationality with COVID-19 or with God

5. Necessity is the mother of invention. In times of crisis, we get creative and resourceful. Many new things are 'birthed'

6. There is an acknowledgement of God and His sovereignty. Despite all our human effort, God always has the final say. Though I say this, the essence of it is that God loves all of us and He desires to have real, meaningful, heart-connected relationship with us, but He wants us to desire it, to come to Him for our love, fulfilment, solutions...He's concerned about everything that concerns us. He's near to all who call on Him

7. We have a whole lot of time to rest, reflect, regroup, spend much needed time with self & family and do those things we 'didn't have time' to do before. Our proximity with those we love is an opportunity to confront issues we may have been avoiding and strengthen those relationships

8. Even the earth is getting a chance to *'ketch itself,'* as our 'lock down' closed factories, parked cars and limited our environment destruction for a time. The earth can breathe again. It's as though the whole world has gotten a reset.

Psalm 145:18
"The LORD is near to all who call upon Him, to all who call upon Him in truth."

A WHOLE NEW WORLD

Being married to Errol has thrust me into a 'whole new world,' a world of discovery and wonder, in some ways, a world that has been going unnoticed or rather, untapped…one in which I'm an anomaly at times.

Yet, I know that this is the sphere to which I am called. I've known that I was called to the mountains of Arts and Entertainment, Media and Government, but I could never envision how God was going to place me there. I'd thought that perhaps it would be through 'the marketplace.' Marriage would never have been the vehicle in my mind, but it seems with this single act, I've been catapulted into them…

ABOUT THE AUTHOR

Jilean Dara-Marie Fabien is an entrepreneur, coach, writer, wife and mother. She discovered her scribal gift as a teenager using writing as a way to vent. Since then, her writing has been used as a way to bring healing to others, motivate and empower, promote and help them to express the things that usually go unsaid.

Jilean is the Owner and Creative Director of JOTBox Ltd., a publishing and expression company and more recently, God Powered Revolution Ltd., a t-shirt and apparel company with a mission to bring transformation through worn expression.

As Destiny Coach, Jilean supports individuals in having harmonious relationships, navigating through life's transitions and their journey to purpose and optimal living.

Jilean can be reached at jilloutthebox@gmail.com

GLOSSARY

WORD	MEANING
Ah mean	I mean
Bazodee	Lightheaded and caught up with someone
Beatin	Beating
Bounced up	Saw someone unexpectedly
Chilo	A nickname for your child
Chupidee	A stupid person
D	The
Doh	Don't
Ent	Not so?/True
Fas'	Fast
Fight me down	To oppose so as to prove wrong
In ting	A part of something special or exclusive
Ketch	Catch
Nah	No, you're kidding
Shudda	Should have
Side Ting	An outside man or woman; An illegitimate relationship
Ting	Thing
Yuh	You

Made in the USA
Coppell, TX
31 March 2024

30670824R10167